ERIN ELLIS

CLASSROOM-READY RESOURCES

FOR

STUDENT-CENTERED LEARNING

BASIC TEACHING STRATEGIES FOR
Fostering Student Ownership,
Agency, and Engagement
IN K-6 CLASSROOMS

ULYSSES PRESS

Published by:
Ulysses Press
PO Box 3440
Berkeley, CA 94703
www.ulyssespress.com

ISBN: 978-1-64604-353-8
Library of Congress Control Number: 2022932301

Printed in the United States by Versa Press
10 9 8 7 6 5 4 3 2 1

Acquisitions editor: Kierra Sondereker
Managing editor: Claire Chun
Editor: Kathy Kaiser
Proofreader: Cathy Cambron
Front cover design: Amy King
Interior design and layout: what!design @ whatweb.com
Artwork: chalkboard (cover) © Hywit Dimyadit/shutterstock.com; raised hands (cover) © Nadya_
    Art/shutterstock.com; page 96 © Tasty_Cat/shutterstock.com

TABLE OF CONTENTS

INTRODUCTION

Let's face it, some days teaching in elementary school feels like trying to herd cats—that is, if the cats talked way too much, constantly needed to use the restroom, and accidentally called you Mom half the time. This often leaves educators in the position of prioritizing. What is my most important task today? We may answer that we want to help our students feel safe and loved, understand and master the content, or learn life skills. Most of us would not often prioritize applying professional development or new strategies, especially on those days when we are confronting a frenzy of cats. But in the case of student-centered education, not applying this approach in our classrooms would be a disservice to our students and to ourselves as well.

Student-centered education developed from constructivist theories on learning. Constructivism started by looking at one of the most important concepts we learn in early childhood: language. We do not learn to speak our native language by sitting behind a desk while a teacher explains it to us. We learn our native language by hearing it modeled and trying it out ourselves. Along the way, we make many mistakes, some of which are corrected for us, but most of which we discover ourselves through our interactions. Our motivation for learning language is predominantly intrinsic, as the applications of language are apparent.

Constructivists looked at learning language as a prime example of individualized learning and wondered why this approach wasn't being used in education. The blending of this theoretical base with the realities of the modern classroom created student-centered learning. In this type of education, rather than all learning originating from the teacher, students are given choices and opportunities to discover and create their own learning. The educator plays a large role by modeling and facilitating problem solving, as well as providing support throughout the learning process. Many teachers have already begun making the shift toward creating a student-centered classroom, and the results speak for themselves.

SUPPORT FOR STUDENT-CENTERED LEARNING

As educators, we want to keep students engaged in learning. Research has shown increased engagement is directly linked with increased student achievement. Student-centered education places great value on engagement and employs many engagement strategies. With this approach, students consistently explore their passions, monitor their learning, and make connections. So it's no surprise that studies have found that greater student engagement, and therefore greater student achievement, are more apt to occur in schools with student-centered learning. A study of four schools that served a large proportion of low-income and minority students found that students who had a student-centered education were more likely to experience several positive effects (Friedlaender et al., 2013). Students who had this type of education were more likely to connect with and find purpose in school. They also were more likely to outperform similar students on standardized tests, graduate from high school, and attend postsecondary schools. Given the achievement gaps among students of different incomes and races in the United States, we must consider what educational methods best address these gaps (Friedlaender et al., 2013).

Another study, this one of more than sixty schools, found that in each school there was a positive effect on student achievement when student-centered learning practices were implemented (Pane et al., 2015). But because student-led learning comes in a variety of shapes and sizes, the size of the positive effect also varies. Schools and classrooms that had the largest and most consistent positive effects were schools that built in important supports to student-led learning. This included providing their students with social-emotional resources and encouraging the development of meaningful relationships between students and teachers. It was also important to have collaborative teamwork among educators so that they could fine-tune their approaches, create new ideas, and compare data. Additionally, schedules allowed for students to work on their explorative or project-based learning for larger blocks of time (Pane et al., 2015).

Specific components of student-centered education have been studied in depth. One such component is personalization. When students' names or interests were included in instruction, direct increases in positive attitudes toward learning, motivation for learning, and demonstration of learning were seen. Student agency is another component of the student-centered approach that has research behind it. Researchers investigated the effects on students who were taught self-regulation and metacognitive strategies. These studies found that students who were taught such strategies exhibited improvements in performance and engagement. As there are many components that could be considered part of a student-centered approach to education, further research is needed to discover exactly what aspects of student-centered education are leading to what benefits (Kaput, 2017).

KEY COMPONENTS OF THE STUDENT-CENTERED APPROACH

The principles of student-centered learning vary with the source. But the general consensus is that student-centered learning should include at least some, if not all, of the following components:

STUDENT OWNERSHIP AND AGENCY. Perhaps the most important tenet of student-centered learning, student ownership and agency are what clearly make education revolve around students as individuals. Creating student ownership of learning requires educators to provide regular opportunities for students to self-assess the progress of their learning, what they are doing well, and what they need to improve upon. Therefore, students must become skilled at metacognition by seeing it modeled and by taking the time to reflect. Student-centered teachers show students what it looks like to think about their learning and recognize the steps that need to be taken to reach their goals. This means that students should be a part of setting goals and the expectations for reaching these goals. In contrast, with teacher-centered learning, students have their goals and expectations dictated to them. Student-centered learning converts goal setting into a collaborative process between students and their teachers, as well as their peers. Along with choosing goals or learning targets, students should also have choices throughout the learning process, whether it be how they convey their learning, what topics they specifically learn about, or the medium by which they learn. Providing chances for choice is the foundation of creating student agency, and thus an important factor in student-led education.

COLLABORATION. Collaborative learning can take place in a variety of manners. Group work, partner projects, peer feedback, and class discussions are all examples of collaboration that student-led learning often uses. Providing opportunities to work with their classmates by one means or another is a large part of getting students to connect with their learning, as well as practice life skills. Students often can explain and provide insight to one another in a way that is more accessible for some students. Collaboration also creates a sense of community, providing a comfortable classroom environment in which students feel a duty to participate. Although group work can be done in a teacher-centered learning environment, with student-centered learning everything is truly student-led. Rather than acting as the sole leader, the teacher helps facilitate and acts as a member of the team.

PERSONALIZATION AND DIFFERENTIATION. The steps educators take based on their knowledge of individual students are the components of personalization and differentiation. With student-led learning, educators may use a student's interests, strengths, or other facets of their identity to personalize the learning experience. Examples include providing a math problem that uses a student's name or putting a group of students together based on their interest in researching the same topic. Differentiation takes personalization deeper. Educators can differentiate the learning contents, processes, products, or environments to meet students' readiness, interests, or learning profile needs. With student-led learning, teachers must have the flexibility to differentiate for student needs. They can meet with students individually or in small groups, make content accessible through multiple media, or give choices regarding the products that students create to demonstrate learning. Educators help students set their own individual goals based on where they are and what they want to accomplish. In this way, every student can grow from their own starting point.

CONNECTION AND APPLICATION OF LEARNING. The element of connection and application of learning is a large factor in what makes student-centered learning not only engage students but also help them attain long-term achievement. Educators introduce problems and skills that both explicitly and implicitly connect to the world outside the classroom. Students can identify why they are learning something and how it is relevant to their lives. For example, math concepts can be introduced that incorporate situations they could encounter in the real world, and reading strategies can be applied to stories about real-life events. In this way, not only do students see the content they are learning as applicable to society, but they also regularly practice life skills. Perhaps the most significant of these life skills is critical thinking. The problem posing and open-ended expression included in student-centered education allow students to gain an ability to problem solve as well as develop a growth mindset.

COMPETENCY-BASED ASSESSMENT. The type of assessments, specifically summative assessments, that we give in our classrooms is sometimes out of our control. Competency-based assessments, however, are a logical inclusion in student-centered education. To gather evidence of what students are understanding and currently capable of, there must be opportunities for students to show their learning. This means excluding most multiple-choice questions and providing options for students to demonstrate their knowledge through various media. Because these are not standardized assessments, many schools find this element the most difficult to apply. But as teachers, we can—where possible—include competency-based assessments in our formative assessments and summative assessments. Schools that used competency-based assessments had better student performance on standardized testing (Bell, 2010). Students were able to truly internalize their learning and critically think.

Some of these components are included in the activities of this book, while others are easy to include in or to use to accompany other activities, based on the needs of your students.

BENEFITS OF IMPLEMENTING STUDENT-CENTERED ACTIVITIES

RELATIONSHIPS. Student-centered learning provides many more opportunities for a student's voice to be heard. This means we, as teachers, can have more insight into who a student is and what they need. Through class discussions, individual conferences, and student collaborative work, you will see more of the whole student and give them feedback to show that you see them as an individual and care about their growth. For many of us, relationships with students are what motivated us to be educators in the first place. But with traditional teacher-centered learning, it can take time out of the school day to develop meaningful relationships with students. In student-centered learning, this bonding time is built in, both between teacher and students and between students. Now that I am using more student-centered practices, I am much more connected with my students and what their capabilities are. I can kindly call students out when they are not giving me their personal best and celebrate with them when they overcome a challenge.

TIME. We all feel the pressure of time in our daily classroom experience. Prior to implementing student-centered learning, I found it difficult to balance the needs of my elementary students with the rigid pace of curriculum and the demands for student performance. In student-centered classrooms, learning takes place anytime and anywhere. Students learn to take initiative and regularly apply their learning across subject areas. This means less hand-holding on the part of the teacher and more time for the teacher to challenge and assist students in purposeful ways. It also means the teacher spends less time explaining the lesson to the entire class and giving direct instruction. Students spend less time relearning. And both teacher and students spend less time practicing for assessments. Once a foundation of solid classroom management is established, students can collaborate and work independently for long periods, leaving the teacher's time available for small-group or individual conferences. At first, educators may have to devote more time to planning. Eventually, though, teachers learn to adapt in the moment to the feedback they receive from their students. Due to this flexibility, educators spend less time outlining a lesson and more time teaching students exactly what they need.

DATA. Data are essential to ensure the efficiency of groups, including classes. The process of student-centered learning provides large amounts of useful student data. Not only are teachers receiving regular information on student progress from formative and summative assessments, but they are also getting data via consistent student self-assessment and communication. These data give the teacher a more complete picture of students' gaps in understanding, strengths and weaknesses, and perspectives. With this information, teachers can better address student needs through instruction and activities. I take the data I am constantly collecting and use it regularly to inform my teaching and to share in teacher team meetings. My data, along with data from my team teachers, create a picture of what is working in our curriculum—and what is not.

ENGAGEMENT. Due to the personalization, differentiation, and general student choice and communication that student-centered learning relies on, students are inherently more engaged in the learning process. Students see their interests and passions in what they are learning. They have a large role in and responsibility for choosing what they learn and how they learn it. They see the application of their learning to their lives. This buy-in to their learning is exactly what keeps students connected to their learning and interested in improving their academic skills and knowledge. I see this all the time, as my students tell me stories about how they used their learning outside the classroom or how they were excited to try something new in their project. We all want to help our students keep a fire burning for their learning, rather than feel like we are dragging them through the coals.

OUTCOMES. Not only do students meet expectations for performance and engage with their learning in student-led classrooms, but they also become more well-rounded individuals. With this approach, students learn to self-reflect and assess, build collaborative relationships, and problem-solve. All these skills are key to students' success inside and outside the classroom. My students confidently navigate unfamiliar situations and try out new ideas. The more student-centered learning a student experiences, the more that student achieves these outcomes.

STUDENT-CENTERED LEARNING

TEACHER-CENTERED LEARNING

- Teacher acts as coach or facilitator of learning
- Students are active in the learning experience
- Students take ownership and responsibility for their learning
- Flexible structure
- Encourages collaboration, self-evaluation, and problem-solving
- Teacher models; students interact

- Teacher is classroom authority figure
- Students are expected to learn

- Teacher acts as lecturer
- Students are passive in the learning experience
- Students are meant to absorb information presented to them in order to learn
- Rigid structure
- Encourages focus on teacher and independent work
- Teacher talks; students listen

CHAPTER 1

WHOLE-GROUP INSTRUCTIONAL ACTIVITIES

At first, when consciously approaching student-centered learning, I felt overwhelmed. How would I make whole-group instruction student-centered? Direct instruction had always been a key component of my whole-group instruction. But after developing and observing student-centered learning activities at the class level, I realized that using student-centered learning in no way meant eliminating direct instruction. In fact, many of the activities included in this chapter involve direct instruction. These activities complement or accompany direct instruction, so students are participants in the learning process.

With the student-centered approach, instruction at the class level allows students to receive information not only from the teacher but also from other students and through their own discovery. Consider professional development days at school. Many times a presenter stands at the front of the room sharing large amounts of information and perhaps posing the occasional question to the entire group. How much of that information do we participants remember? How many times do we actually take much of what we have been presented with and use it in our classrooms? Probably not as much as we, or our principals, would like. If we do not learn best in this environment, then our elementary-age students surely do not.

Student-centered whole-group instruction involves everyone as a participant in the learning process. With this approach, direct instruction empowers students by giving them the tools, strategies, and mindset to approach the learning target. The instructional activities in this chapter all use or can accompany this type of direct instruction. They involve the entire class in an adaptive learning process.

MODEL MINI-LESSON

In the model mini-lesson, the teacher teaches a brief lesson in which they model for students the ways that students could go about approaching the task, strategy, or content at hand. The goal of the mini-lesson is to empower students so they feel confident attempting the skill on their own following the lesson.

TIME: 5 to 15 minutes

POSSIBLE MATERIALS: Mentor text or example task, anchor chart

COMMON APPLICATIONS: Mathematics, reading comprehension and analysis, writing process and skills

Step-by-Step Guide

1. Provide an anticipatory set, one that connects what you will be teaching to life outside the classroom. This can be an anecdote, an interesting fact, or even a brief video or song.

2. Review the learning target or goal, that is, what you want students to be able to do after the mini-lesson. Make a direct connection between the target and the anticipatory set.

   • If the learning target is one previously discussed, reiterate the expectations for what it would look like to meet the goal.

3. Model a specific strategy or concept using the mentor text or example task (4 to 8 minutes). Accompany modeling with a visual aid or anchor chart and walk through the task while verbally conveying what you are thinking as you go through the process. Address thought processes students could have and common mistakes they might make. As you do so, make sure to include students' names, interests, and so on, to personalize the lesson. This step often requires materials or resources that you want students to be familiar with or use during their learning.

4. Provide a minute for students to either ask questions or discuss (with a partner, a small group, or the whole group) what they observed.

5. Give students a task or mission to which they can apply what they just saw modeled.

6. Review the learning target and the main ideas you want students to remember before dismissing students to complete their task or mission.

Teacher Prompts

- When I see this, I might think _____.

- I try to start by _____ because _____.

- I wonder if _____.

- What if I try _____?

- I can see that _____.

- I don't understand why _____.

- Now I see that _____.

- This makes sense because _____.

VARIATIONS

- Give students a task or mission before the mini-lesson, give them time to work independently or through small-scale collaboration, and then review the specific task or mission through the mini-lesson.

- Allow a student to lead part of the mini-lesson by modeling their thinking as they go through a process.

Classroom Case Example

Mrs. Stuart calls her second-graders to the classroom's front carpet area for a reading mini-lesson. Once everyone is settled and focused, she begins with a short anecdote.

"All right, as you know, I have a daughter, Brianna." The class nods in agreement. "And Brianna loves to watch *SpongeBob SquarePants*. Two characters are Brianna's favorites. One is Sandy the Squirrel and the other is Patrick Star. One day I asked Brianna which was her favorite, Sandy or Patrick. She said she didn't know, but she began listing all the reasons she liked Sandy, all the reasons she liked Patrick, and all the reasons she liked them both. Brianna was comparing and contrasting without even realizing it.

"Put your hand up if you have heard those words before: *compare* and *contrast*." Mrs. Stuart pauses as some students raise their hands. "So some of us have already heard of those words. Well, today our goal is to compare. We want to be able to compare two characters from our reading." Then Mrs. Stuart has the students read aloud with her the learning target she has written on her anchor chart: I can compare two characters.

Mrs. Stuart continues, "So what does it mean to compare?" She gives students a few seconds to think before asking everyone to whisper their answer out loud to the class. Then she tells the class what she heard and uses these answers to define what it means to compare, writing students' responses on the paper as she goes. Mrs. Stuart then draws a Venn diagram on the chart paper. She explains that this is a Venn diagram, its purpose, and how our story today has two main characters, Lola and Mitch. She writes the two names on each side of the Venn diagram and says that each has a side to himself or herself for things that are true about only that character.

"We will use these parts of the Venn diagram when we learn to contrast these two characters, but today we are going to focus on the middle, where we are going to write down things the characters have in common." She pulls up a few pages from the story on the front screen. Mrs. Stuart has chosen these pages because they include dialogue and actions that show commonalities between the two characters. She begins reading the excerpt aloud to the class. After a couple of paragraphs, she pauses and speaks her thoughts aloud. "I noticed that Lola is speaking very kindly to the new student in the story and is offering to help a lot. She says 'thank you' and 'please.' This tells me that Lola is probably a friendly, kind, and polite character. I wonder if our other character, Mitch, will be the same way."

Mrs. Stuart continues reading aloud. Reaching her next stopping point she says, "As I read how Mitch invited the new student to play and made her laugh by burping the alphabet, I was thinking this was good evidence for how Mitch is as a character. He's being friendly, kind, and funny." Mrs. Stuart then turns back to her Venn diagram. "So if I am focusing only on comparing my two characters, then I want to list only what they have in common. Lola is friendly, kind, and polite. Mitch is also friendly and kind, but I didn't have any evidence for him being polite. I think I'll list just *friendly* and *kind* in the middle of my Venn diagram.

"I want you to notice that I listed character traits that were the same. Characters can also have the same likes, such as baseball, or the same experiences, such as both being in second grade. But I wanted to make sure I was digging deep, so I was focusing on listing things about who the characters are." Mrs. Stuart then asks the class to think about how they would answer these questions: What does it mean to compare two characters? How do you compare them? After a short amount of think time, she asks students to turn to their assigned carpet partner and share their answers. After students have begun wrapping up the discussion, Mrs. Stuart asks for someone to share their answers with the class.

"We said that comparing is finding out how the characters are the same," one student answers.

"And how would you find out how the characters are the same?" Mrs. Stuart asks.

"By thinking about how they act the same and what they are like," the student replies.

"Exactly," Mrs. Stuart says and smiles. "Now I have a mission for all of you today. I am going to give you some time to go read on your own. You will need to find a fiction book with at least two characters. I want you to draw a Venn diagram just like I have up here and include the names of your two characters." She points to where she has done the same. "Then I want you to list in the middle how those two characters are the same. You are going to compare them by finding evidence or examples in your book of how they are alike. Think about how those characters act and think and what they say.

"Are you ready for your mission? Does anyone have a question?" Mrs. Stuart waits some time to make sure the students don't have any questions. She sees students' heads nodding. "All right, go get focused on your mission!" Students stand up, get their supplies, and settle into reading.

ANCHOR TASK

The anchor task allows students to develop their problem-solving skills and growth mindset. Students are given a task that they are somewhat unfamiliar with or may find challenging. They then have a brief amount of time to try to complete the task independently without much instruction. Afterward, the class discusses methods or strategies they used to attempt the task. This anchor task allows students to feel comfortable and capable when attempting to solve novel problems.

TIME: 15 to 45 minutes

POSSIBLE MATERIALS: Student workspace materials (that is, personal whiteboards, paper, online document), presentable anchor task

COMMON APPLICATIONS: Mathematics, reading comprehension and analysis, scientific investigation, writing skills

Step-by-Step Guide

I. Ensure students have the materials necessary to complete the task.

2. Present a brief anchor problem or task, usually one that attempts to draw upon students' prior knowledge. Make sure the task can be completed in more than one way or has more than one answer.

3. Give students time to attempt to complete the task. Provide a backup task or prompt for students who finish well before the others.

4. Move throughout the classroom to provide positive feedback, make minor suggestions, and verify that all students are making their best attempt.

5. Regain students' attention once the majority of students have completed the task.

6. Allow several students to share out or demonstrate not only their completed task but also their process for completing that task. Hand off as much or as little explanation as you like to the students.

7. Give time for students to process or discuss the task further.

8. Review the various approaches used and their strengths.

Teacher Prompts

- What do we know about _____?
- Can you try another way?
- I love how you are trying more than one strategy.
- Let's think about what it's asking.
- There is more than one way to think about this.
- You started by _____.
- I see, you tried to do this by _____.

VARIATIONS

- Use the anchor task to review previously taught tasks that haven't been visited for a while.
- Give students the same task or similar tasks several days in a row to make students more comfortable with the multiple ways to attempt a task and discover what is most efficient.
- Share in partners or small groups first or instead of a whole-group share-out.

Classroom Case Example

Mr. Keller is getting ready to teach his fourth-graders two-digit multiplication. He gets the students' attention and ensures they have their whiteboard and supplies ready at their seats. Then he asks if students remember what the word *product* means. Students give various answers before one student says, "It's the answer to a multiplication problem."

Mr. Keller acknowledges that this is the type of product students will be working with today. He reminds students that they have solved multiplication problems before. This time, he says, they will be finding the product of a two-digit number multiplied by a single-digit number.

"In a second, I'm going to put a problem on the board. You may not have solved a problem exactly like this before, but I want you to try your best, and use what you already know, to attempt this. Everyone should be able to come up with at least one strategy, and maybe more, for solving this problem."

Mr. Keller then presents a brief word problem on the board. He reads it aloud to the group and tells them to take their time to try to solve the problem. He also states that if they solve the problem with one strategy, then they should try another strategy or multiple other strategies.

"Each of you should be working the entire time to understand what the problem is asking and solve the problem using as many strategies as you can," Mr. Keller says. "Now please begin working."

The students uncap their markers, ponder the question, and begin solving the problem in various ways on their whiteboards. Mr. Keller circulates throughout the room. He pauses to give students praise, such as "Thanks for trying another strategy" or "I love that you wrote out the equation," just loud enough for students nearby to hear and apply his comments to their own work. He also stops to help his struggling students find a good starting point and his successful students to get motivated to attempt the problem another way.

After about six minutes of work time, Mr. Keller asks students to set their markers down. He then asks four students, each with a different strategy, to come to the front of the room with their whiteboards. He asks them to stand in a particular order. The student farthest to the left is the one with the most literal, least efficient take on the problem. The student farthest to the right is the one with the most abstract, most efficient strategy. One by one, each student at the front flips their board over, and Mr. Keller asks the class to identify what strategy the student used and how well it worked.

"First, let's look at Claudia's board. What strategy did Claudia use to solve this problem?"

Students answer that she drew a model or picture.

"Yes, exactly! Claudia drew a model that allowed her to visualize the problem in order to solve it. This is a wonderful way to start to understand what the problem is asking and solve it. So how did Claudia lay out her model?" Mr. Keller probes. He calls on a student.

"Claudia drew six equal groups, each with the label of forty-five cupcakes. So she knew that she could add each of the groups of forty-five together to get how many cupcakes there were in all," the classmate explains.

Mr. Keller picks back up: "Yes, so we can see that Claudia used her model to repeatedly add the groups together to find the answer. This strategy is great for seeing our problem and helping us write our equation. But it can take a while to add each group as we start getting into larger numbers. Thank you, Claudia, for sharing with us. Let's take a look at Jakoby's board. What strategy did Jakoby use?"

Mr. Keller leads this process for each of the student examples. He presents these strategies in this order so that students can see the connections between strategies. Each can be used to solve the problem and has certain key elements that are the same. He wants his students to be able to find a strategy that works well for them and yet be challenged to at least understand how other strategies may work to solve the same problem.

When all the strategies have been shared and discussed, Mr. Keller prompts the students to talk with their table partners about what strategies they feel comfortable with and what strategies might be most efficient. After students have the opportunity to discuss with their partners, they are asked to share out with the class. The class reviews the strengths of each strategy, when or who it might be best used by, and its level of efficiency. Now the class can move on to a new problem with a clearer idea of what strategies they can use.

THE GREAT MISTAKE

The Great Mistake allows students to attempt a task that they've practiced during prior class time. Once students are given a brief task, they complete the task and return it to the teacher, who quickly sorts through students' work, searching for an example of good work with a commonly made mistake. The teacher presents this example to spark a class discussion of the mistake, why it was made, and how to avoid it in the future.

TIME: 10 to 15 minutes

POSSIBLE MATERIALS: Index cards, notebook paper, or a Jamboard (for online work), document camera or whiteboard

COMMON APPLICATIONS: Mathematics, reading comprehension and analysis, spelling, writing skills

Step-by-Step Guide

1. Ensure that students have the proper materials, such as index cards, notebook paper, or a Jamboard, to work on the given task.

2. Present a small task or problem on which students are making a common mistake.

3. Give students a few minutes to complete the task.

4. Have students signal when they complete the task.

5. Collect students' work once they finish it and pick out an example with a commonly made mistake.

   • Ensure students know what to work on while they wait for others to finish.

6. Get the attention of the class and show them the first example with a mistake using a document camera or by copying it onto the whiteboard. Do not share the student's name.

7. Ask students to find what the example did well or correctly and briefly discuss.

8. Ask students to find the specific mistake in the example and why it may have been made.

9. Share the reasons the mistake demonstrates an understanding of the task at hand despite it being the incorrect outcome.

10. Discuss how to prevent the mistake in the future.

11. Repeat if desired for other common mistakes.

Teacher Prompts

• This is a wonderful mistake because _____.

• What was this learner trying to do?

• I love this mistake because _____.

• Often when we try this, we _____, which makes sense, but _____.

• What can we do to prevent this mistake in the future?

- Why did this mistake happen?

- Mistakes make the brain grow.

- I've made this mistake by thinking _____.

Classroom Case Example

Ms. Sanchez's sixth-grade science class has been learning how to draw atoms using the periodic table. Ms. Sanchez hands out index cards to the students. She then displays the periodic table and asks students to draw an atom of nitrogen on their index cards.

"When you have completed your drawing, please give me a thumbs-up so I can collect your index card. Once I have collected your card, you should read silently."

Students begin working on the task. As Ms. Sanchez collects the index cards, she notices that some students are using the mass number as the entire number of neutrons, rather than subtracting the atomic number from the rounded mass number. She looks for a well-drawn example with this mistake while she finishes collecting student work.

Once she has collected all the students' index cards, Ms. Sanchez gets the attention of the class. Then she begins by reiterating the given task.

"I asked the class to draw an atom of nitrogen for me. You all did a wonderful job using the information on the periodic table to help you complete your drawing. Here is one of the examples I loved seeing today." Ms. Sanchez places her chosen index card under the document camera.

"What did the student who drew this atom do well?" Ms. Sanchez asks the class. Classmates answer that the student used the atomic number to draw the correct number of protons and electrons and that the example has all the parts of the atom in the correct location.

"I agree," comments Ms. Sanchez, "that it was clear the student was using the periodic table to find the atomic number of nitrogen. They also remembered where to place each of the different particles within the atom." Ms. Sanchez continues: "What mistake did this student make when drawing the nitrogen atom?"

Students answer that there is an incorrect number of neutrons. Ms. Sanchez asks for more information. "Where did they get the number of neutrons?"

"They used the mass number rounded to the nearest whole number, as they are supposed to, but they forgot to subtract the number of protons. Because protons and neutrons are the particles with mass, they both make up the mass number," a student explains.

"Thank you, Jeremy, for that detailed explanation. We use the mass number to determine the number of neutrons. But, as Jeremy said, because protons and neutrons have mass, we have to subtract the number of protons the atomic number gives us from the rounded mass number. So how many neutrons should we have?"

"Seven," the class answers.

"Right," replies Ms. Sanchez. "If our rounded mass number is fourteen, and our number of protons from the atomic number is seven, then the number of neutrons must be seven as well."

"I chose this mistake because I could tell the student was really paying attention to the information in the periodic table. They also knew that the number of neutrons comes from the mass number, which is important to remember. They simply forgot to subtract the number of protons to be left with the number of neutrons."

Ms. Sanchez wraps up by asking students if they have any questions about drawing atoms or their particles.

RUBRIC CREATION

To create a rubric, a class works together to determine the key components of a final product. Although the teacher has a general idea of what should be included in the rubric, students help define the expectations based on their learning targets. The result is not only students' ownership of what their final products should include, but also a clear understanding by students of what it takes to create high-quality work.

TIME: 20 to 60 minutes (may last several class sessions)

POSSIBLE MATERIALS: Rubric document (see below) or anchor chart, learning targets, Bloom's taxonomy/verbiage

COMMON APPLICATIONS: Any content area projects, any content area written explanations or pieces, any content area performance tasks

	MASTERY CRITERIA 4	PROFICIENCY CRITERIA 3	DEVELOPING CRITERIA 2	EMERGING CRITERIA 1
Learning Target:				

Step-by-Step Guide

1. Present a learning target worked on for a set unit or lesson.

2. Record the learning target on the rubric document or anchor chart.

3. Analyze and explain as a group what the learning target means.

4. Collaborate to answer the question: What are the criteria for success? Determine what the specific expectations would be to reach a mastery level of the learning target. Do the same with the expectations for proficiency, developing, and emerging levels.

- Use example products, if they can provide more clarity.

5. Record these expectations on the rubric.

6. Repeat if multiple learning targets are being addressed.

Teacher Prompts

- What would it look like to master (to be proficient at, to be developing, to have just started working toward) this learning target?

- How can we tell that you understood the learning goal?

- How would you demonstrate your learning?

- When I think about the word _____, I know that means that you can _____.

- What should I look for to know that you understand this?

- If I can [learning target], I can _____.

Classroom Case Example

Kindergartners in Mr. Martin's classroom are gathered at the front of the room. Mr. Martin reminds the students that they have been learning how to write the numbers 0 through 20.

"You have been working so hard to learn how to write the numbers 0 to 20. Soon I will be asking you to write all of these numbers down for me. Let's talk about what will let me know you understand how to write these numbers," Mr. Martin begins. He points to a rubric grid on the front board. "This is a rubric. We are going to fill in the parts of this rubric together. This rubric will tell you exactly what it takes to show me that you know all of your numbers from 0 to 20."

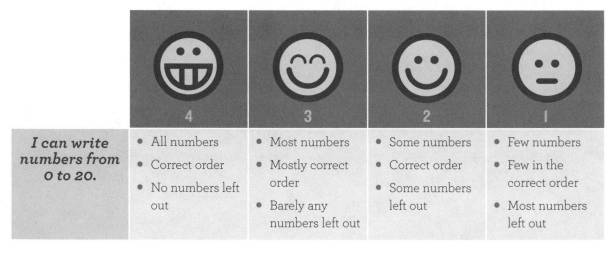

I can write numbers from 0 to 20.	4	3	2	1
	• All numbers • Correct order • No numbers left out	• Most numbers • Mostly correct order • Barely any numbers left out	• Some numbers • Correct order • Some numbers left out	• Few numbers • Few in the correct order • Most numbers left out

Mr. Martin asks the class what their learning target is again. When they answer, he adds this learning target to the rubric: "I can write numbers from 0 to 20."

Then Mr. Martin asks the class, "What would it look like to write numbers from 0 to 20? What would it look like to reach this goal?" He calls on a number of students, who variously answer, "Writing the numbers, not letters," "Writing all the numbers," and "Counting in order."

"Wonderful," Mr. Martin replies. "So you're telling me that to show me you can write these numbers you need to write actual numbers with the correct number shape, include all of them, and write them in the right order? Is that something we think each of us can eventually do?" Mr. Martin gives each student time to nod or respond yes.

"Okay then! Let's add that to the rubric," Mr. Martin says as he adds the list to the mastery section of the rubric. He reiterates what each point means so that students have a clear understanding of what the expectation is for mastery.

"All right, so now we know what it will look like to show me that you fully know how to write your numbers from 0 to 20. What about if you just mostly know? What will it look like to be able to pretty much write your numbers from 0 to 20?"

Mr. Martin calls on students to respond. He gets a variety of answers, but he can connect most of them to the ideas that have already been placed on the rubric. "So what I think you are saying is that the difference between this level on our rubric and the first level is that you would make a few mistakes, such as using the wrong shape for a couple of numbers, leaving out a couple of numbers, or putting the numbers down in a slightly wrong order." The students nod, and Mr. Martin adds these criteria to the rubric.

"So now we need to figure out what it would be like to only kind of show me that you can write your numbers from 0 to 20. Turn to your floor partner and take turns sharing what you think it would look like to only partly be able to write your numbers from 0 to 20. The person who has the longer hair will share first, and the person with the shorter hair will listen first. Share now."

After giving students time to share, Mr. Martin asks some partners to share out. He then adds to the rubric the expectations the class has discussed in relation to the previous criteria. He repeats this process with the class for the final criterion level. Mr. Martin wraps up the rubric creation by summarizing what the rubric includes and how it will be useful in the future.

"We will be using this rubric as we do our practice count-outs so you can see exactly what I will expect from you. Thank you for helping me figure out what it looks like to be able to write your numbers from 0 to 20."

EXEMPLAR ANALYSIS

This activity allows the class to view final products as a whole group, before working on or completing the product individually. The goal of this exemplar analysis is for students to understand which products demonstrate sufficient learning and growth and which do not. Students can apply this understanding when creating and polishing their learning products.

TIME: 5 to 20 minutes

POSSIBLE MATERIALS: Examples of student work, mentor texts, or both; rubric

COMMON APPLICATIONS: Any content area projects, any content area written explanations or pieces, any content area performance tasks

Step-by-Step Guide

1. Determine the options for final products your students will be asked to create.

2. Find an example or examples of this product from previous student work, a mentor text, or elsewhere.

   - At least one should be an example of ideal work.

3. Provide the example to the class along with the rubric or other scoring material.

4. Prompt students to look at particular attributes of the piece in accordance with the rubric or scoring material.

5. Discuss with specificity why the example would receive a given rubric score or another rating.

6. Repeat with multiple examples for more clarity of rubric expectations.

Teacher Prompts

- What do you notice?

- What do you think was done well in this example?

- What could have been done better in this example?

- What do you think you can apply to your own work?

- How do you think this example would score on _____?

- If this were your work, what would you hope someone would tell you?

- Overall, what kind of example is this?

VARIATIONS

- Use concurrently with rubric creation to provide examples while elements of the rubric are being formulated.

- Give the examples to small groups of students first, and then have them gather to discuss with the whole group.

- Complete this activity while students are creating the product, not just when introducing it, to exemplify specific criteria individually.

Classroom Case Example

Miss Pimm's fifth-graders are going to be writing scientific explanations soon. Their goal is to write a three-part explanation that includes making a claim, providing evidence, and giving reasoning. To help her students understand what she will expect from them, Miss Pimm wants to show them a few examples of student work. First, she hangs up an enlarged copy of the rubric for scientific explanations. Miss Pimm wants to focus today's exemplar analysis on one specific criterion from the rubric: I can give evidence to support my claim. Miss Pimm starts by reviewing the rubric scoring levels in detail for this criterion. After this she introduces the activity the group will be completing together.

"We will be using this rubric to score three examples of student work. This is work I have received from previous students, and each of them has something different we can look at to learn from," Miss Pimm explains. "Let's start with this one," she says while putting a less-than-ideal example up on the screen. She reads through the example. Then she reminds everyone what their task is. "What do you notice? I'll give you a minute to think about what you have noticed. Remember, I want us to pay close attention to how this student did regarding the goal of providing evidence."

After giving students a minute of "think" time, Miss Pimm asks students to share what they noticed with their table group. Then she calls on one person from each group to share their group's thoughts. Once every group has shared, Miss Pimm summarizes what they said. "So what I'm hearing from you is that this student did a nice job providing one piece of evidence in connection with the claim but did not provide enough evidence to meet the goal." Students nod. "Okay, show me on your fingers what score you think that would be on our rubric." Most students hold up a two or three out of the five-point scale.

"I'm seeing mostly twos and threes," Miss Pimm responds. "I agree. I gave this student a two because there was not enough evidence to support all parts of the claim. Our goal, as the rubric says, is to provide at least three pieces of evidence for the claim. Let's look at another example."

Miss Pimm pulls up another piece, which is an example of ideal student work. She has students repeat the same process of noticing, group discussion, and finger scoring. This time students give a general rating of fours and fives. "I gave this example a five because they provided three pieces of evidence and connected each to the claim," Miss Pimm explains, while pointing to the parts of the example she's referencing.

Finally, Miss Pimm repeats the process with her class one last time. This time it is with an example that is middle of the road. Miss Pimm is using this example both because it represents the quality of work she most often receives from students and because she wants students to be able to distinguish between the highest level of work and the level right below it.

Once all discussion has been held about the final example, Miss Pimm briefly compares and contrasts the examples. Then she introduces the task students will be completing to practice offering evidence for a claim.

LARGE-SCALE PEER FEEDBACK

This activity presents the class with current examples, anonymous or not, of students' in-progress work. Class members analyze the material, provide positive feedback, and suggest possible areas of improvement. Students gather ideas for how to improve their work, gain collaboration skills, and learn to accept compliments and criticism alike.

TIME: 5 to 20 minutes

POSSIBLE MATERIALS: Feedback anchor chart, rubric, document camera/uploaded images/ online work

COMMON APPLICATIONS: Any content area projects, any content area written explanations or pieces

Feedback Anchor Chart Example

I CAN PROVIDE HELPFUL FEEDBACK.		
Classy Compliments	AND	Specific Suggestions
I like how you...		How would you feel about adding...
My favorite part was...because....		I'm unclear on how you...
I can tell you really worked hard on...		Maybe there is a better way to...

You used...really well		I think you could add/take out...because...
The strongest part was...because...		One suggestion I have is...
I enjoyed...		I think...could be even better if...
I noticed you....		I noticed you...

Step-by-Step Guide

1. Ask for volunteers or pull anonymous student assignments to show works in progress.

2. Remind students of expectations for the assignment via a rubric or other means.

3. Present student work for all to see or provide individual copies.

4. Give students time to view all parts of the work.

   - You may ask the individual whose piece you are presenting if they want help with anything specific.

   - Read the information aloud, especially with younger grades, to ensure students get through the content at a similar pace.

5. Go over the expectations for feedback verbally or by using a feedback anchor chart.

6. Have students share specific positive things they notice about the work.

7. Have students share specific areas for improvement they notice and also suggest how to make these improvements.

8. If they have not done so already, help students connect the feedback with the rubric by referencing specific criteria that relate to the feedback.

9. Repeat this process for one or two other student pieces.

Teacher Prompts

- What specifically do you notice that this student has been making great progress on?
- What are the strengths of this piece?
- Are there areas that could be improved upon?
- What would you suggest this student add or change?

- Can you be more specific about what you noticed?

- Let's provide some suggestions for how this student could make these improvements.

Classroom Case Example

Students in Mr. Phillips's second-grade class have been creating miniature stores for their economics unit. Students most recently have been developing advertisements for their stores. Advertisements can be in a variety of media and are expected to include the names of the items or types of items the store sells, mention the name of the store, and grab the audience's attention. As students have already had some time to work on their advertisements, Mr. Phillips wants students to see examples of other students' work, as well as receive feedback.

Mr. Phillips gathers the students together at the front of the room. He asks if anyone would like to share their current advertisement with the class. Mr. Phillips chooses one of the volunteers and pulls up their video advertisement on the front screen. Before playing the video for the class, Mr. Phillips references the sign hanging up that has a list of "what effective advertisements include." After briefly reviewing this with the class, he instructs them to keep these elements in mind as they watch the video advertisement.

Mr. Phillips then plays the video advertisement. As this is meant to be a stand-alone piece, he does not ask for the student whose piece this is to provide any information. Rather, Mr. Phillips dives right into asking the class for feedback. First, he asks students to share what they noticed the advertisement did well. After several students share, he prompts students to share what could make the advertisement more effective.

Finally, Mr. Phillips connects the feedback from the class with the criterion list for advertisements. He reiterates what the advertisement did well and how it could be improved with regard to the criterion list. Mr. Phillips thanks the student for volunteering to share and has the class give a small celebration for them.

Mr. Phillips repeats this process with two more students' advertisements. He chooses volunteers who have used different media, so the class can see how the various platforms can all be used to meet the criteria. Again, when the student is finished sharing Mr. Phillips acknowledges the student gratefully and has the class give another celebration.

CLASS MEETING OR DISCUSSION

A class meeting or discussion has a wide variety of applications. This group session can be used to address an issue at hand, break apart a concept, or expose students to new ideas. It is best used with learning targets and topics that have multiple possible approaches and outcomes to help students see a wider picture.

TIME: 20 to 40 minutes

POSSIBLE MATERIALS: Sharing or talking stick, expectations or comments anchor chart

COMMON APPLICATIONS: Reading analysis, scientific discussions, social-emotional learning, social studies debates, writing brainstorming

Expectations or Comments Anchor Chart Example

BE READY TO...		
Sit silently	Silently sit and listen to speaker	
Hand raise	Raise your hand to share after someone has finished speaking	
Awesome attitude	Keep a positive attitude during discussion	
Respect others	Use respectful words when sharing	
Engage	Pay attention to what is being said, look at the speaker, and be ready to respond	

Step-by-Step Guide

1. Have students sit in a circle, either on the floor or at their desks. Make sure there is a spot for you as well.

2. Go over the expectations for sharing and listening within this setting.

   - If using a sharing or talking stick or other object, include this in the expectations.

3. Introduce the problem or topic for discussion.

4. Prompt students to discuss the why or what of the problem or topic.

   - Allow each student a chance to speak if they would like.

5. Ask students to provide solutions or explanations for the problem or topic and build upon each other's ideas.

6. Help transition between students and connect ideas when necessary.

7. Finish on a positive or clear takeaway.

Teacher Prompts

- What could be causing _____ to happen?

- What is your reasoning?

- Can someone build upon that for us?

- What are the possibilities here?

- Is anyone willing to share their point of view?

- Let's come up with some ideas for _____.

- Thank you for sharing that _____. Does anyone want to respond to what this student just said?

VARIATIONS

- Make the class meeting a "share circle" by not bringing up any issues or prompts in particular and allowing students to pick the topics for discussion.

- Give a student the role of meeting leader or facilitator to allow students even more ownership of the process.

Classroom Case Example

Mrs. King has noticed a recurring issue with her first-grade students interrupting each other during one-on-one or small group conversations. She wants to hold a class meeting to help students discuss and problem-solve this issue. She has students come to the learning rug and form a circle. Once students are sitting calmly in a circle, she explains the expectations she has for a class meeting.

"We are going to have a class meeting," she says. "In our class meetings, everyone will have the chance to share if they would like. But unless you are Mrs. King, you cannot speak unless you have this stuffed animal. This is Talking T. rex. This stuffed animal will be passed gently around the circle so everyone can share their ideas. Eventually, even I won't speak unless I have the Talking T. rex, but for now, I am going to help you learn how a class meeting works."

Now Mrs. King introduces the problem. "I've noticed a lot of us have been struggling with listening carefully to others when we are talking with our friends. We have been interrupting or talking over others when they are speaking or about to say something.

"Let's start by talking about if you have noticed this as well and how it makes you feel. We aren't naming names or pointing fingers. We are simply talking about the problem as a whole because it seems to be happening with many of us. I'm going to pass the Talking T. rex to my left, and we are going to just pass it around the circle. If you don't want to share, just keep passing it. If you do want to share what you think or feel about the interrupting issue, please share quickly so everyone has a chance to speak."

As the T. rex is passed around the circle, some students share their feelings and thoughts. Many students share that they feel sad, upset, or angry when they get interrupted. Mrs. King often asks students to elaborate.

"Can you tell us why being interrupted upsets you?" Mrs. King asks. Students give various reasons, but ultimately it comes down to feeling that their classmates are not listening. Once every student has had a chance to share their feelings, Mrs. King reiterates this.

"Many of us have shared how being interrupted makes us feel. Everyone who shared said that being interrupted does not make them feel good because they don't feel listened to. So let's talk about why interrupting is happening, so maybe we can figure out how to solve the problem. Does anyone have an idea of why the problem is occurring? If so, please raise your hand."

"I see Lilah may have an idea. Can we please pass the T. rex to Lilah?" Mrs. King says. Once several students have shared their reasoning, Mrs. King summarizes again.

"Thank you for sharing. From what I am hearing, it sounds as though we are not meaning to interrupt others most of the time. Instead, we are so excited to tell them something that we speak before we know whether they are through sharing. How do we think we can solve this problem?"

Mrs. King has the Talking T. rex passed to several students to share. A few students have silly solutions, such as raising a hand before speaking in a personal conversation, so Mrs. King respectfully questions their practicality. But some students suggest waiting patiently so they know their friends are done talking before they themselves start speaking.

Mrs. King adds a little to this solution. "I love the idea of making sure we wait until our friend is finished speaking. I think this will help a lot if we think about it while we are in a conversation. But we are going to need some practice with this, and we may make mistakes. What do you think we could say to someone if they interrupt us accidentally?"

A few students give suggestions, and Mrs. King feels that this is the time to conclude the class meeting. "Does everyone agree? Can we try to think more about whether we are interrupting each other, and say something respectful as a reminder if we are interrupted? This way, we can all feel happier and more comfortable in our classroom." Students nod in agreement, and Mrs. King begins transitioning her students to the next thing in their day.

INQUIRY-BASED LEARNING

Inquiry-based learning comes in a variety of shapes and sizes. The goal of this activity or string of activities is to allow students to explore possible solutions or answers to an open-ended question. Students build upon their exploration and research to further develop their understanding of a concept as well as their skills.

TIME: Can range from a 20-minute lesson to an entire 2-to-6-week instructional unit

POSSIBLE MATERIALS: Journals or recording tools, question chart

COMMON APPLICATIONS: Making inferences, mathematical patterns and concepts, scientific exploration, word and spelling patterns

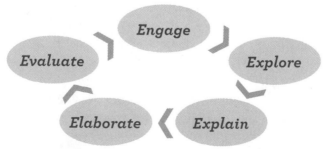

Step-by-Step Guide

1. Pose a large, open-ended question. Present the question and any related or investigative questions on a chart within the room.

2. Engage students by introducing a related phenomenon or issue that is not immediately explicable to them.

3. Provide students with the opportunity to explore what may be causing the phenomenon or possible solutions to the issue. Have students record their observations, thoughts, and findings using a journal or tool.

4. Allow students to explain their theories.

5. Provide another similar circumstance to allow students to test their theories.

6. Ask students to evaluate whether their theory can still apply or how it has changed.

7. Remind students of the original question. Ask them to attempt to answer it, knowing what they now know.

8. Repeat the process if necessary to uncover more details to answer the initial question.

Teacher Prompts

- What do you think causes this to occur?
- How could we uncover what is behind this?
- You are going to explore _____.
- Let's figure out how this happens.
- After learning more, how does this change how you look at this phenomenon?
- How does this pattern apply to other instances?
- What other circumstances can we connect this situation to?
- Are we noticing any patterns?

Classroom Case Example

Mrs. Tonkovic wants her fifth-grade students to explore the elements of art. She begins by posing her overarching question to the group: "What makes something art?" Mrs. Tonkovic explains that during their next few class sessions, she wants students to explore what it means for something to be art. Then she pulls up a piece by Salvador Dali.

"This is considered art," she says, "but what makes it so? What makes this art? I want you to investigate and formulate ideas for the next twenty minutes on what makes this piece art."

Mrs. Tonkovic then gives the class time to explore the piece by Dali via online research and observation. She provides several specific resources for them as a starting point. After students have finished their exploration, Mrs. Tonkovic asks students to record their thoughts on what makes the Dali piece art. The students share their current ideas in a brief class discussion on what makes this art.

Mrs. Tonkovic repeats this process with the class over several class periods. Each time she presents a new piece of artwork drastically different from the previous one. Students begin piecing together different elements that all the pieces have in common. At the end of the several sessions of exploration, Mrs. Tonkovic asks the class to define and explain the necessary elements of art.

POSTER SLAPS

This activity allows students to have their ideas heard and to expand their thoughts on an introductory topic or project. Students go to either physical or electronic posters or pages to add their thoughts or answers about a category of the topic or a question on the topic. Eventually, these ideas are shared out and discussed, providing alternative ways of thinking about the topic.

TIME: 10 to 15 minutes

POSSIBLE MATERIALS: Chart paper or Padlet (for online learning), sticky notes, markers or other "fun" writing utensils

COMMON APPLICATIONS: Any content area generating ideas, social-emotional learning

Step-by-Step Guide

1. Hang up several poster pages around the room for students to write their ideas on.

2. Introduce the overall topic or learning target of the posters.

3. Provide writing utensils, and possibly sticky notes, to students. They will use these to record their thoughts on each page's prompt. They will either stick the notes on or write their ideas directly on the page.

4. Challenge students to make it to every poster and put at least one new idea on it in the time given. Students who record on every poster once should go back to add another idea to some other posters.

   - Clarify that this means they should read what has already been said so they do not duplicate what another student has recorded. You may ask students to put a mark, such as a star, next to ideas that they agree with or would have written themselves.

5. Gather students together and bring the posters to the front of the room.

6. Read out to the class what was recorded for each prompt.

   - Spark a discussion about each useful idea.

7. Leave posters someplace visible, so that they can be referred to for any applicable upcoming work or lessons.

Teacher Prompts

- What immediately comes to mind?

- Are there any ideas already written that you can build on?

- Think about what this can apply to.

- How do you see this?

- What's the most unique, creative, or interesting idea you can think of regarding this topic?

VARIATIONS

- Use an online document or interface instead of physical posters.

- Create prompts to review a topic rather than introduce it or brainstorm for it.

Classroom Case Example

Mr. Meyer's fourth grade is learning about and writing nonfiction. He wants to help students expand their ideas about possible topics within this genre. Mr. Meyer places several large pieces of paper around the room with topic categories, such as historical events, celebrities, animals, and scientific discoveries. On some of the more difficult categories, he has already written an example. Mr. Meyer asks students to each grab a marker. Then he has students gather as a group.

"Today our goal is to generate ideas for nonfiction writing topics," he begins. He explains that fifteen different posters have been hung around the room to help students brainstorm topic ideas. "Each poster has a category for you to record at least one writing topic idea. The challenge is you cannot repeat what anyone else has already put on the poster, so you need to read through the ideas before adding your own. Because there are so many posters, there shouldn't be more than two or three students writing on a poster at one time. If you see there are already two or three of your peers at one poster, go to a different one." Mr. Meyer models this process and then releases students to find a poster to help them start generating ideas. As students are pondering writing ideas, Mr. Meyer circulates throughout the room, prompting students to help them generate ideas for a specific category.

Once Mr. Meyer sees that most students have made it to each poster at least once, he gathers them together again and asks students near each poster to bring them to the front of the room. With all the posters hanging on the front board, it is easy for students to see just how many writing ideas they can choose from. Mr. Meyer reads some example ideas out loud to the class.

"Now I want you to go back to your writing journal and jot down at least five of these nonfiction topics, or others you came up with, that you would be interested in writing about. Then choose one of your favorites and begin to outline what you want to say about it." Mr. Meyer dismisses students to begin their independent work.

Tips for Success: Setting Up Whole-Group Instruction That Works for You

STRATEGIC SEATING. Be conscious of whom students are sitting near, not only for behaviors, but also for academic and social strengths. If you typically have students at their table or desk during lessons, you probably already have them strategically placed. But if you ask students to come to the floor space in the room, you may not. I assign carpet partners for discussion. Though these partners change fairly frequently, students know whom to turn to during any particular discussion, so I do not have to spend time making sure everyone is paired up. You can even give the partners a fun name, such as your school colors or food pairings (for example, Blue and Gold Partners or Chips and Salsa Partners).

NONVERBAL SIGNALS. Give students ways to participate in class discussion nonverbally. There are many options for hand signals that can help whole-class communication. I personally have students use signals for agreeing and disagreeing, levels of understanding, and wanting a turn to share. Not only do signals limit disruptions in class discussions, but they also give a voice to those students who may be less willing to share verbally.

MAKE TIME LIMITS OBVIOUS. If an instructional activity has a time limit at any point, present a visual timer or give multiple verbal warnings. This eliminates some of the stress students might feel about getting work done. I find that when tasks have time limits, giving a visual representation limits the number of questions about the time remaining and empowers my students to learn time management skills. That said, you must express the value of doing something to the best of one's ability rather than rushing. I always tell my students I would rather they not finish something but turn in work that is their absolute best, as opposed to rushing to finish and turning in work that isn't a true representation of their capability.

VISUAL AIDS AND ANCHOR CHARTS. Be intentional in the creation of visual aids and anchor charts. These tools must be thoroughly explained, grade-level appropriate, and succinct. They can be incredibly useful in creating visual memories and tools for students to use when working independently—but do not overwhelm students with too many visual stimuli. I usually place the learning targets on my visual aids so students know to reference them in relation to specific goals.

CHAPTER 2

SMALL-GROUP INSTRUCTIONAL ACTIVITIES

Meeting with students in a small group can be extremely effective and efficient student-centered instruction. Learning in a small group is more personalized and relationship-driven. Students have their voices heard at a level that may be more comfortable for them while being held even more accountable than usual. Meeting with students in small groups creates the perfect balance between collaborative learning, independent work, and teacher instruction.

A variety of methods may be used to group students according to needs and interests. Determining how you want to group students may depend on the type of small-group activity you are implementing, its purposes, and how often the small group will meet.

GROUPING BY RECENT FORMATIVE ASSESSMENT DATA. Using recent formative assessment data can help you group students according to similar gaps in understanding so that you can help them fill in these gaps and meet learning targets.

GROUPING BY PRE-ASSESSMENT DATA. Preassessment data can help you identify students who are already proficient. Grouping these students together can allow you to provide them with enrichment or extension activities to keep them engaged in learning.

GROUPING BY POST-ASSESSMENT DATA. Using post-assessment data to group students can allow you to review and reteach students who have yet to master the learning targets.

GROUPING BY INDIVIDUAL GOALS. Placing students with the same or similar individual goals in the same small group can allow you to teach them strategies and present them with opportunities to make progress toward their goals.

GROUPING BY INTEREST. Working with a small group of students who have similar interests can provide you with more opportunities to personalize small-group activities and thus increase engagement.

GROUPING BY STRENGTHS AND WEAKNESSES. You may choose to put a small group together based on self-identified or observable strengths and weaknesses. You might group together students who share the same strengths or weakness in order to address the area. On the other hand, you might group together students with a variety of strengths and weaknesses so they can learn from each other.

If you are intentional in your use of small groups, they can allow students to bridge gaps in understanding and attain proficiency or mastery of the content at hand. In this chapter, you will find a few activities for the small-group setting. These activities are versatile in subject application but are meant to address students who have been grouped with thought and data. If you implement a typical small-group schedule for certain subjects, you might plan to use a variety of these activities across multiple sessions with the same small group.

SMALL-SCALE PEER FEEDBACK

Similar to large-scale peer feedback, this activity presents the small group with students' current works in progress or performance. The group analyzes the material or performance, provides positive feedback, and gives suggestions for possible areas of improvement. Students gather ideas for how to improve their work, gain collaboration skills, and learn to accept both compliments and criticism.

TIME: 5 to 25 minutes

POSSIBLE MATERIALS: Feedback anchor chart (see page 28), rubric, student work

COMMON APPLICATIONS: Any content area projects, any content area written explanations or pieces, performance tasks (such as reading with expression)

Step-by-Step Guide

1. Instruct every student in the small group to bring their current works in progress to your group meeting.

- Alternatively, provide a performance task for them to complete at the beginning of the group meeting.

2. Remind students of expectations for the assignment or performance via a rubric or other means.

3. Allow an individual student to present their work to the group.

4. Give the other students time to view all parts of the work.

- You may ask the individual who is presenting if they want help with anything specific.

5. Go over the expectations for feedback verbally or by using a feedback anchor chart.

6. Have students share specific positive observations they have of the work.

7. Have students share specific areas for improvement they notice and give suggestions for how to make these improvements.

8. Help students connect the feedback with the rubric by referencing specific criteria in relation to the feedback if students did not do so already.

9. Repeat this process for the rest of the members of the small group.

- This can be done throughout multiple group meetings.

Teacher Prompts

- What specifically do we notice that this student has been making great progress on?

- What are the strengths of this piece or performance?

- Are there areas that could be improved upon?

- What would you suggest they add or change?

- Can you be more specific about what you noticed?

- Let's provide some suggestions for how they could make these improvements.

Classroom Case Example

Ms. Compton's first grade has been working on drafting a writing piece. Students have chosen what to write about, and they have recently had lessons that modeled for them how to incorporate illustrations in their writing. Ms. Compton notices that a few students are struggling with the illustrations, including either too many illustrations, too few illustrations, sloppy illustrations, or illustrations that don't truly pair with the written story. She pulls these students over to her back table to discuss their writing pieces. Once all five students are settled, Ms. Compton explains why they are meeting.

"We've been working on creating illustrations, or pictures, that add to your story. I pulled us together today to listen to a few of your stories and take a look at the illustrations that you have drawn with them." Ms. Compton then reiterates the expectations she has taught about what good illustrations are, using the rubric she has lying in front of her. Next, she asks for a volunteer to share their writing with the group. Ms. Compton picks a volunteer, Britta, to share her story and illustrations with the group. After Britta is finished sharing, Ms. Compton lays the writing piece out on the table for everyone to see. She briefly states the expectations the group has for providing feedback as displayed on an anchor chart.

"What do we notice that Britta did well, especially when it comes to her illustrations?" Ms. Compton asks. After getting a few positive points of feedback, Ms. Compton asks what Britta could do to improve her writing piece, focusing especially on illustrations. Ms. Compton helps her first-graders provide feedback that ties into the rubric.

"Britta, we loved how you used illustrations that matched nicely with what you were writing about on each page. We think you could go back to some of your illustrations to add in a little more color or detail to be more interesting to the reader," Ms. Compton summarizes. "Group, thank you so much for sharing. Britta, we can't wait to see your finished piece!"

The group repeats this process with the rest of the group to help its members understand how they could change their illustrations to meet the expectations set out in the rubric.

ENRICHMENT SMALL GROUP

In an enrichment small group, students who have already mastered a learning concept can build on or explore similar concepts with peers so that learning is still applicable and engaging to them. This can provide them with the tools to continue challenging themselves and collaborate with peers who may think differently about how to accomplish something.

TIME: 10 to 20 minutes

POSSIBLE MATERIALS: Student workspace materials (that is, personal whiteboards, paper, online document), practice problems, examples, exploration or learning sources

COMMON APPLICATIONS: Mathematical concepts, science or social studies content

Step-by-Step Guide

1. Identify a current class concept that several students have mastered, but with which the rest of the class still needs practice.

2. Determine a facet or further iteration of this concept that you will not be introducing to the entire class during the school year.

3. Gather the group of students who have mastered the initial concept in a small-group session.

4. Reiterate the learning target the whole class has been working on and its significance.

5. Introduce the new facet of this learning concept via a short lesson or example.

6. Provide time during the small-group session for students to try out or explore the concept using practice problems or examples, and workspace materials.

7. Assign students a project, game, practice, or other source that allows them to work with this newly introduced facet of the concept.

Teacher Prompts

- This concept also has an application in _____.

- Once we have mastered this concept, we can begin to look at _____.

- I am going to challenge you to use what you have learned about this concept to work on a new type of problem or task.

- Have you ever thought about what this might look like if we used it with _____?

- What more do you want to know about _____?

VARIATIONS

- Identify multiple new facets of the concept and allow students to choose in what direction they would like to take their enrichment work.

- Instead of making this an enrichment group, you can make it an extension group by giving students more challenging ways to apply the initial concept.

Classroom Case Example

Miss Nguyen's third grade has been learning about forces and motion in their current science unit. Most of the class are still working on conceptualizing what a force is and how forces act in the world. But a few of Miss Nguyen's students demonstrated mastery of this content on the most recent formative assessment. After assigning the rest of the class an independent exploration activity, Miss Nguyen pulls these four students to meet with her.

She begins by reiterating what the students already know about what a force is and how it works. She then tells students that in their small group they will be discussing two specific forces: gravity and friction. Gravity will be discussed briefly with the whole class during later lessons, but friction will not be mentioned at all. Miss Nguyen shows the small group a video about both forces. Then she offers some of her own examples.

After introducing the two forces, she asks students to come up with examples of when gravity and friction are acting on objects. The group discusses each example so they can further conceptualize how the two forces work. Miss Nguyen makes this a time of open discussion so students can present thoughts or ask questions.

Finally, Miss Nguyen presents students with the choices they have for the remainder of science time. They can create a book, an online presentation, or a website to teach others what friction and gravity are and when they occur in the world. Miss Nguyen provides students with several reference resources and sends them on their way.

MODEL MINI-LESSON

The enrichment small-group model mini-lesson is similar to a classwide model mini-lesson, with the instructor teaching a brief lesson demonstrating the metacognition and approach behind a strategy or skill. The goal is to empower students to apply the same type of metacognition and approach in their work. The small-group model mini-lesson can also be used to reteach a concept to students who need reinforcement.

TIME: 5 to 15 minutes

POSSIBLE MATERIALS: Mentor text or example task, anchor chart or paper, student workspace materials (that is, personal whiteboards, paper, online document)

COMMON APPLICATIONS: Mathematics, reading comprehension and analysis, writing process and skills

Step-by-Step Guide

1. Provide an anticipatory set, one that connects the lesson to life outside the classroom. This can be an anecdote, an interesting fact, or even a brief video or song.

2. Review the learning target or goal, that is, what you want students to be able to do after the mini-lesson. Make a direct connection between the target and the anticipatory set.

   - If the learning target is one previously discussed, reiterate the expectations of what it would look like to meet the goal.

3. Briefly model a specific strategy or concept using the mentor text or example task (4 to 8 minutes). Accompany modeling with a visual aid or anchor chart, and walk through the task while verbally conveying what you are thinking. Address thought processes that students could have and common mistakes they might make. As you are doing so, include students' names, interests, and so on, to personalize the lesson. This step often requires materials or resources that you want students to be familiar with or use during their learning.

4. Provide a minute for students to either ask questions or discuss with the small group what they observed.

5. Give students a task or mission in which they can apply what they just saw modeled.

6. Review the learning target and the main ideas you want students to remember before dismissing students to complete their task or mission, either while still in the small group or independently.

Teacher Prompts

- When I see this, I might think _____.

- I try to start by _____ because _____.

- I wonder if _____?

- What if I try _____?

- I can see that _____.

- I don't understand why _____.

- Now I see that _____.

- This makes sense because _____.

VARIATIONS

- Start the small-group session by giving students a specific task or mission before the mini-lesson. Then use the mini-lesson to go over the task or mission.

- Allow a student to lead part of the mini-lesson by modeling their thinking as they go through a process.

Classroom Case Example

Mr. Green has been teaching his fifth-grade English class about figurative language. He has noticed that differentiating between imagery, similes, and metaphors has been difficult for a handful of students. He pulls these students to meet with him and presents them each with the lyrics to a popular song. The lyrics include examples of the three types of figurative language.

To begin the small-group session, Mr. Green gets students engaged by discussing the background of the song they have in front of them. He talks about who wrote it and who performed it, and then he talks about how the song makes great use of figurative language.

"Our goal is to be able to see or hear written words and be able to tell if the writer is using imagery, simile, or metaphor in any given phrase," Mr. Green explains. He then references an anchor chart they have been using in class to explain what these three types of figurative language are and show an example of each.

STRATEGIC SMALL GROUP

Within a strategy group, students who have not yet mastered a learning concept are introduced to new strategies or further scaffolding of a concept that was not introduced at the whole-group level. The teacher groups students with similar areas of needs to help them address these needs with the group lesson and practice.

TIME: 10 to 30 minutes

POSSIBLE MATERIALS: Manipulatives or learning tools, student workspace materials (that is, personal whiteboards, paper, online document)

COMMON APPLICATIONS: Any content area with varying approaches or strategies, any concept with well-defined scaffolding

Step-by-Step Guide

1. Gather a small group of students who are having difficulty keeping up with the strategies introduced in whole-group instruction.

2. Introduce a new method or a further broken down strategy to approach the same concept.

- This strategy could be one that was introduced in previous grade levels.

3. Give students time to practice the strategy with teacher assistance and appropriate tools or materials.

4. Monitor the effect of the strategy on student progress toward the learning target.

Teacher Prompts

- Another way to think about this is _____.
- Let's revisit how you did this in a previous grade.
- We're going to take this together step-by-step.
- When I look at this, I can consider using this tool.
- What strategy might work most efficiently for you?

VARIATION

- For students who have a strategy that works for the given task but is no longer efficient for the current level of work, use this small group to help them use a more efficient approach.

Classroom Case Example

Mr. Kim has been teaching his class how to round to the nearest 10, 100, and 1,000. Much of this has been review from previous grade levels. But a few of his students are struggling to consistently round to the correct 10s place. To help these students reach proficiency, Mr. Kim pulls them into a small-group session.

In this session, Mr. Kim provides students with a 100s chart. He explains how to use the chart to help determine which two 10s a number is between, as well as which one the number will round to. Mr. Kim models this a couple of times. Then he gives the small group a few practice problems. He walks them through the initial attempts and then allows them to try it on their own, assisting when needed.

Mr. Kim wraps up the group session by giving students one problem to try completely independently using the 100s chart. Once every student has completed the problem, Mr. Kim reviews it with the group, reiterating the steps it takes to use a 100s chart to round to the nearest 10.

Tips for Success: Setting Up Small-Group Instruction That Works Well for You

ESTABLISH A NORM. Make small-group instruction a typical part of your classroom routine. This doesn't necessarily mean having a regularly scheduled time for small groups, although that can be beneficial. Rather, it means making it commonplace for students to be pulled over into a small group. Small-group instruction is more effective if students have a regular experience with the small-group setting. They know the expectations for a small-group meeting, and they do not feel singled out or shamed for being part of a small-group session.

VARY THE ROSTERS. Change the composition of the small groups throughout the school year. If you have small groups that meet regularly to work toward the same goal, try to rearrange these groups every quarter or so. Varying who works in a group allows students more opportunities to work with and learn from all their classmates. It is also beneficial for student morale. If certain students are always pulled together, this may create the impression that they are performing either particularly poorly or well in a specific area. Changing group composition allows students to focus on challenging themselves to learn.

OUTLINE EACH SESSION. Small-group sessions should be planned, just as you would plan whole-group instruction. Student-centered learning allows for this planning to be an outline, rather than a rigid plan, because the trajectory of each session will depend on student discussion and performance. But the general direction of the session must be planned, as well as the time frame, so that each meeting is a productive use of class time.

BE CONSCIOUS OF SMALL-GROUP SIZE. Think carefully about how many students you will place in a small group. Too many students means students get inadequate attention and assistance, but too few students is an ineffective use of time. A rule of thumb is three to six students, with the ideal being four or five.

FIT THE NEED. If you notice that most of your students require reteaching, enrichment, or specific strategy help, small groups may not be the right solution. Use whole-group instruction when most of your class has the same or a similar need. Small groups are best used to address the needs of a small set of students.

CHAPTER 3

INDIVIDUAL CONFERRING ACTIVITIES

One-on-one conferring is a luxury in teaching. We often don't have enough time to implement individual conferring activities in our classrooms as much as we might wish. But the practice of teacher–student conferring is one that not only helps build the relationship between student and teacher but also allows us to address specific student needs. It is a quintessential example of a student-centered practice that meets the student at their individual level. But as the only collaboration during a conference is between the teacher and one student, be conscious not to use conferring for something that could be more effectively done in a whole-group or a small-group setting.

Each of the conference activities in this chapter has a specific purpose. But all conferences are an ideal method of passing the baton to students. Working one-on-one with students, you can empower them to take ownership of their learning goals, thought processes, and demonstrations of learning. Conferences also provide an excellent time to build a working teacher–student relationship.

GOAL-SETTING CONFERENCE

In a goal-setting conference, the student and teacher meet to help the student establish an individual goal and determine the steps needed to meet this goal. The student is the primary decision maker, with the teacher providing the expertise needed to make the goal attainable and the steps productive.

TIME: 5 to 10 minutes

POSSIBLE MATERIALS: Goal record sheet, student data

COMMON APPLICATIONS: Any content area with measurable growth, mathematical problem-solving goals, reading strategy application or skill goals, writing strategy application or skill goals, social-emotional goals

Goal Record Sheet Example

MY GOAL	
Goal:	
Steps I will take to achieve this goal:	
Self-Assessment 1	What will I do next to make progress toward my goal?
Date:	
Circle where you are at toward meeting this goal: 4: I can complete this goal independently and teach someone else how to as well 3: I can complete this goal without help 2: I can complete this goal with some help 1: I can complete this goal with a lot of help 0: I can start on this goal with help	

Self-Assessment 2	What will I do next to make progress toward my goal?
Date:	
4: I can complete this goal independently and teach someone else how to as well	
3: I can complete this goal without help	
2: I can complete this goal with some help	
1: I can complete this goal with a lot of help	
0: I can start on this goal with help	

Self-Assessment 3	What will I do next to make progress toward my goal?
Date:	
4: I can complete this goal independently and teach someone else how to as well	
3: I can complete this goal without help	
2: I can complete this goal with some help	
1: I can complete this goal with a lot of help	
0: I can start on this goal with help	

Step-by-Step Guide

1. Determine the parameters or area within which you want students to set a personal goal.

2. Meet with a student individually and outline the goal-setting parameters or area.

3. Ask the student what goal they think they should work toward next.

- Possibly provide a list of example goals to help them determine their own goal.

4. Discuss whether their choice of goal would be an appropriate goal for them and why.

5. Have the student record the goal.

6. Brainstorm together the steps to take to achieve this goal or how it will be determined that the goal has been met.

7. Record this information as well.

8. Place the recorded goal and steps somewhere accessible to the student and yourself.

- Consider making a copy or displaying this information on a bulletin board, so that this goal is accessible to both parties.

Teacher Prompts

- What do you want to get better at in this area?

- Where do you think you can make growth?

- What steps will you need to take to make this happen?

- How will we know that you have met this goal?

- What can I do to help you meet this goal?

- Is this something you are passionate about accomplishing?

VARIATIONS

- Prompt students to set individual goals during whole-group instruction. Then meet with students to solidify these goals.

- Set goals in a small-group session, and give each student time to confer with you individually within the session.

Classroom Case Example

Ms. Spring is meeting with her students individually to help them set their personal reading goals. Before conferring with the students, Ms. Spring has explained to the class what a reading goal should be. When she meets with her student Pablo, she reiterates these expectations.

"We are going to be setting your reading goal together today. Remember, your reading goal should be something you want to work toward with your reading. It should be something you truly need to grow toward." Ms. Spring then presents Pablo with a list of possible goals she has used with other students. She reads through the list with Pablo and helps him understand what each goal means.

"This is just an example list of goals. Are there any goals from this list, or that you can think of on your own, that would be a good fit for you?" Ms. Spring asks. Pablo points to this goal: "I can read with expression." Ms. Spring asks Pablo why he thinks this would be a good goal for him. Once Pablo has explained, Ms. Spring agrees and hands him a goal record sheet. She asks him to write down this goal.

Next, Ms. Spring asks Pablo what he thinks needs to happen for him to achieve his goal. Together Ms. Spring and Pablo talk through what it would look like for him to read with expression, how he can work toward this goal on his own, and how Ms. Spring can give him tools to help him in future conferences or small-group sessions. They record these items on the goal record sheet.

"I am so excited to help you reach this goal. Are you glad you picked this goal?" Ms. Spring says to Pablo. Once they have wrapped up, Ms. Spring explains to Pablo that she has put his goal in her records as well and has him put the goal record sheet in the goals section of his binder.

CHECK-IN CONFERENCE

In a check-in conference, the teacher and student meet to discuss a student's self-assessment, reflection, or performance. They monitor student progress, provide evidence of progress, and explain how progress occurred (or did not occur). Then the next steps are determined to help the student continue working toward the goal or achieve the goal.

TIME: 2 to 10 minutes

POSSIBLE MATERIALS: Goal record sheet (see page 52), self-assessment sheet (that is, star and steps, rubric), student data

COMMON APPLICATIONS: Any content area with measurable growth, mathematical problem-solving goals, reading strategy application or skill goals, writing strategy application or skill goals, social-emotional goals

Star and Steps Example

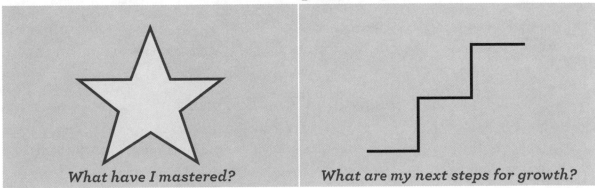

What have I mastered?   *What are my next steps for growth?*

Step-by-Step Guide

1. Meet individually with a student, with their recorded goal present.

2. Together with the student, review their goal and all that it entails, as well as any of their current data.

3. Ask the student to assess their progress toward the goal using a self-assessment or self-reflection tool.

4. Determine or reiterate the next steps toward the goal the student should take.

   - If the student has met the goal, have a mini-celebration instead.

5. Ensure that the student has a record of their goal and the next steps.

Teacher Prompts

- What goal are you working toward?

- What progress do you think you have made toward the goal so far?

- What do you think you still need to do to accomplish this goal?

- What can I do to help you achieve this goal?

- Thank you for taking the time to determine how you are going to meet your goal.

VARIATIONS

- Have students self-assess prior to meeting with you and discuss the self-assessment once you meet.

- Meet with a student regarding a whole-class goal or learning target (one that they may not have a separately recorded goal for) to discuss their progress toward that goal.

Classroom Case Example

Coach Richards is going to confer with his students about their individual physical education goals. Each of them has set a goal regarding effort, perseverance, or sportsmanship. Coach Richards calls over his student Jackson to meet about his goal of being kind to others even when he's frustrated.

Together the two look at Jackson's goal, which is hanging on the gymnasium wall. On the poster, underneath Jackson's goal, there is a "star and steps" self-assessment graphic organizer. Coach Richards prompts Jackson to share what he feels he has mastered regarding his goal. Jackson says that he feels he is getting better at not using mean words when he gets frustrated while playing.

"I agree," says Coach Richards. "You've done a wonderful job not making rude comments to your classmates during PE anymore. That's a great step toward reaching your goal." Jackson records this in the star on his poster. Coach Richards prompts him to continue the self-reflection: "What do you think are your next steps toward reaching your goal of being kind?"

Jackson takes some time to think. He struggles to brainstorm what he could do next, so Coach Richards lends him a little assistance. He reminds Jackson that sometimes he has kicked the ball away from a classmate, and one time he even shoved another student.

"Would you consider those actions kind?" Coach Richards asks Jackson. He responds that they are not. So Coach Richards suggests that Jackson's next steps be something to help him be kind with his actions, not just his words. He has Jackson put the next steps in his own words. Jackson states that he will try to keep control over his body and let out his frustrations without hurting people. Coach Richards agrees with this goal and helps Jackson put it on the next steps part of his poster.

ROLE REVERSAL CONFERENCE

The role reversal conference allows the teacher and student to practice a skill. During the conference, the teacher acts as the student by working through a skill, and the student acts as the teacher by helping them catch their mistakes, as well as coaching them. Students begin gaining the skills for mastery by identifying missteps and teaching another how to complete a process.

TIME: 5 to 10 minutes

POSSIBLE MATERIALS: Student and teacher workspace materials (that is, whiteboards, devices), anchor charts or other instructional tools or aids

COMMON APPLICATIONS: Grammatical practice, mathematics, reading strategies

Step-by-Step Guide

1. Determine a concept with which a student is familiar but needs more practice to master it.

2. Meet with the student and introduce the premise of switching roles.

3. Ask the student to monitor you as you complete a practice attempt of the concept, making one or two intentional mistakes.

   - You may wish to reference an anchor chart or other instructional aid to remind the student of what the ideal outcome should include.

4. Have the student give you specific feedback on what you did well and what you might have done incorrectly.

5. Request that the student coach you on how to remedy your mistakes.

6. Repeat with multiple practice scenarios if that would be beneficial.

Teacher Prompts

- Is this the correct next step?

- What did I do well?

- Where might I have made a mistake?

- Is there a tool you can show me to help me with this?

- Can you help me understand why that is?

- Walk me through this, please.

VARIATIONS

- Rather than making mistakes, act like a robot in a conference with a student. Tell the student you cannot do anything until they tell you specifically what to do, one step at a time.

- Before switching roles, have the student complete a similar task. Coach them on their mistakes so they have a recent model as reference.

Classroom Case Example

Miss Crenshaw has been working with her first-graders on the sounds *g* can represent. One of her first-grade students, Taylor, has been making a few mistakes while reading with a small group. Taylor has trouble telling when *g* represents the /g/ sound and when it represents the /j/ sound. Miss Crenshaw pulls Taylor for a conference. She explains that they are going to switch roles. She is going to act like the student and read a short passage, while Taylor listens and helps her as the teacher.

Miss Crenshaw gives Taylor her own copy of the passage and begins reading as the student from Taylor's copy. As she reads, she makes an intentional mistake with the word *gym*. Using context clues and spelling rules, Taylor can tell Miss Crenshaw has said the word incorrectly. They tell Miss Crenshaw how the word should be pronounced.

"Can you help me understand why what I said was wrong?" Miss Crenshaw prompts her student. Taylor explains that because the story is about basketball, it would make sense for the word to be *gym* with a /g/ sound. "So what if I saw this word just on its own? How would I know it's supposed to be said this way?" Miss Crenshaw questions.

Taylor responds that we can test how the word is said by trying it with both a /g/ and a /j/ sound, and then determining if either one is a word we've heard before. Though this is correct, Miss Crenshaw has also taught her students about the general rule that g can say /j/ only if it is followed by an e, i, or y. She shows Taylor a small anchor chart with this rule. Taylor looks over the chart and realizes what they can add to their feedback. After explaining to Miss Crenshaw that because *gym* has a y after the g, the g could make a /j/ sound, Taylor seems to be grasping the whole picture. Miss Crenshaw gets out another practice passage to go through the process one more time, and she makes some slightly different intentional mistakes.

COMPLIMENT SANDWICH CONFERENCE

Sandwich conferences are a quick way for teachers to touch base with their students on an individual level. Students either perform a task or present their work quickly to the teacher. The teacher provides three pieces of feedback to the student: first a specific compliment, and then a suggestion for improvement, and finally another compliment. The student gains confidence in what they are doing well while receiving a clear direction for the next steps.

TIME: 2 to 5 minutes

POSSIBLE MATERIALS: Sticky notes, list of common feedback options

COMMON APPLICATIONS: Displays of mathematical explanations or work, independent reading, reading comprehension or reflection, independent writing, written explanations

Step-by-Step Guide

1. Approach a student who is attempting a process or task.

2. Observe or listen to them explain how they are working on the task.

3. Give them three pieces of specific feedback, either verbally or in writing on a sticky note, or both.

   - The first piece of feedback should be a compliment.

   - The second piece of feedback should be constructive criticism.

   - The third piece of feedback should be another compliment.

4. Leave the student to absorb and apply this feedback.

Teacher Prompts

- I love how you _____.

- The way that you _____ was very beneficial because _____.

- I think if you were to make this small change it would _____.

- I'd like to see you _____.

- Can you try _____?

- Something I noticed was _____.

- What a wonderful job you did _____.

VARIATIONS

- If you are short on time, just have a compliment conference in which you give the student one compliment on how they are completing the task. This will build their confidence and your relationship.

- Record your compliment sandwich on a student's turned-in work and confer with them to discuss it.

Classroom Case Example

"Hi, Jaelyn," Mr. Torres says as he pulls up a chair beside one of his students. "Can you walk me through how you are solving this problem right now?" Jaelyn responds that she read the problem, drew a rectangle, and labeled its length and width. Then she started adding up the sides to find the area.

"The way you drew a model of the problem and labeled the side lengths is super beneficial. What a great way to start solving the problem!" Mr. Torres compliments her. He continues, "I noticed you may have switched up perimeter and area. We need to multiply length and width to find the area. Can we try multiplying these two numbers to solve the problem?" Jaelyn nods.

Mr. Torres wraps up by saying, "I love how you included the units of meters in your work so you can use it in your solution. Keep it up!" With that, Mr. Torres leaves Jaelyn to continue problem-solving.

Tips for Success: Conferring in a Productive, Efficient Manner

CHOOSE YOUR SETTING THROUGH TRIAL AND ERROR. Try conferring in multiple settings in your classroom. You might find it more productive to go to students individually. Alternatively, you might prefer to have them come to you at your desk or a table. Your choice of setting might depend on the type of conference you will have. There are benefits to all settings, so find what works best for you.

BE DIRECT. Students typically love receiving one-on-one attention from a teacher. But this often leads them to attempt to avoid the task at hand. Be direct about your expectations for the conference and keep the student on track. If you engage in brief small talk, make it clear when you have transitioned to work, using your tone and body language.

PLAN WHO, WHAT, WHEN, WHERE, AND WHY. It can be extremely beneficial to plan whom you are going to confer with each day, what you will confer with them about, when and how long will you confer, where this conference will take place, and why you will hold this conference (that is, your goals for this conference). For example, if you would like to confer with each of your students to set their initial reading goal, you might plan to use twenty-five minutes of each day of a five-day school week to confer with them. You can plan out the five students you will meet with each day and have your watch on hand to ensure each conference is about five minutes long. Planning out how you will structure your conference time allows you not only to be more efficient but also to accommodate all your students.

START WITH A SCRIPT. Conferences are short so that you can confer with every student within a given time frame. To convey your thoughts during a conference, it can help to either have a script for yourself or a list of feedback options to provide to the student. This way you are being clear, concise, and consistent in how you convey important ideas. Each conference will vary greatly according to the student. But having a list of possible phrases, prompts, or feedback can allow you to feel more comfortable adapting to the student's needs in the moment.

SPECIFIC GOALS LOCATION. Consider designating a location for all students to keep their individual goals. This could be at their name tag on their desk, in a binder or notebook, or on a bulletin board. In my classroom, I have a board where students use a sticky note to post their individual goals for each area. A self-assessment tool is next to each of their goals. Use what works well for you and your students but keep consistent for each subject so students know exactly where to find their stated goals while working toward meeting them.

CHAPTER 4

COLLABORATIVE LEARNING ACTIVITIES

Although whole-group and small-group instruction include elements of collaboration, collaborative learning activities are completely student-led. Students work together without the teacher sitting in on or leading every part of the process. Collaborative learning activities are a surefire way to provide one of the key tenets of student-centered learning: engagement. But as a new teacher, I hesitated to implement collaborative learning in my classroom because of the noise, arguments, and time off task that accompanied this approach. But I soon realized that clamor, conflict, and small distractions were all part of a healthy classroom, just as they were part of a healthy adult workplace. I also realized that there were plenty of ways to provide structure to collaborative learning activities so that every student had an excellent learning experience.

Various methods can be used to form collaborative learning groups. Teachers commonly select groups using student preferences or strengths. This method allows the teacher to use what is already known about students to form groups who will work well together. Students may also be allowed to form groups on their own without any prompting from the teacher. The risks of this approach are that student groups could be imbalanced and unproductive. Alternatively, a middle-ground approach is for students to self-group within some parameters set forth by the teacher.

The ways that students are grouped can have an impact on their learning and goal achievement. You might have some ideas about how each student will behave in a group setting, but student behavior might change based on the peers with whom they are working. Normally reserved students might be more likely to speak up when working with those students who are kind and inclusive, or those with whom they already have good relationships. In contrast, students with similar interests or relationships outside the classroom might be easily distracted and drawn off topic when working together, especially if they are all outgoing.

JIGSAW

In a jigsaw activity, students are grouped and assigned a role. They complete the assigned duties of their role and meet up to share with others from different groups who share the same role. Finally, they rejoin their original group to teach the group what they have learned. Each student is responsible for becoming an expert on the duties of their role and then teaching that role to their initial group.

TIME: 30 to 90 minutes (may last several class sessions)

POSSIBLE MATERIALS: Research tools or resources

COMMON APPLICATIONS: Social studies subtopics, science subtopics, reading or writing categories

Step-by-Step Guide

1. Determine the number of subtopics you want students to learn about.

2. Group students together in small groups. There should be enough students in each group to cover the number of subtopics you have outlined. For example, if there are seven subtopics, each group should have seven members.

3. Assign each student in a group a different subtopic to research.

4. Give students the time and means to research and record what they learn about the subtopic.

5. Allow students with the same subtopic to meet and discuss as a group what they have learned.

6. Have students return to their original group and share what they have learned about their subtopic.

Teacher Prompts

- What do you want to know about your subtopic?

- What ideas can you share with your group that might be new for them?

- What could you learn that would benefit your group?

- How can you present what you have learned in an understandable manner?

- What new information did you gain?

- What information was the same or similar for everyone?

VARIATIONS

- Students in a small group are each assigned their own topic, but do not meet with a group of students who have the same topic before sharing with their original group.

- Students in a small group are all assigned the same topic and work together to research it. They then present what they have learned to the entire class.

Classroom Case Example

Fourth-graders in Miss Taney's class are learning about the regions of the United States. The class has been introduced to the five US regions and their locations. Their learning target is to be able to identify specific characteristics of each region. Using a student preference survey, Miss Taney has assigned each student the region of their choice. Each student has also been placed with a group of students, each of whom has a different region.

Miss Taney introduces their jigsaw task. Students will use a variety of resources, including an online research database, a digital library, a physical library, and a video, to learn about their region. Students are given a record sheet, which includes broad categories, such as climate and culture, for them to take notes on their research. After going over the resources and giving examples, Miss Taney releases the class to do their research.

Throughout a couple of class sessions, students have had the opportunity to complete their research. Now students group up with other students who have been researching the same region. They discuss the information they have found, ensure their information is not contradictory, and add what others learned to their own information. Miss Taney also prompts the students to highlight or star as a group what they believe to be the most important information about their region.

Next, students switch back to their original group. They present the important information for their region to their group. Group members have a question-and-answer session before the next group member shares.

ACCOUNTABILITY STATIONS

Accountability centers or stations are activities in which students work together to complete various tasks, producing some sort of evidence of learning after one or all stations. Students work together to explore a topic and demonstrate their understanding.

TIME: 10 to 25 minutes per station

POSSIBLE MATERIALS: Bins or sets of supplies, student devices, instructional signs

COMMON APPLICATIONS: Skill practice in any subject, application of related skills

Step-by-Step Guide

1. Determine the number of stations and groups for effective collaboration and for the desired outcome at each station in the time allotted.

2. Map out where each station will be located and the direction in which students will move between stations.

3. Provide clear instructional signs, plentiful supplies, and a means for the collection of work at each station.

4. Thoughtfully group students into partnerships or small groups.

5. Briefly explain each station as well as how and when students will move between stations.

6. Go over collaboration expectations.

7. Give students time to complete the task at each station.

Teacher Prompts

- How could you coach someone on this?
- Have you tried problem-solving with your team?
- How might you and your partners think about this differently from each other?
- What do you not understand yet? Does one of your partners understand it?
- How can you work through this together?

Classroom Case Example

Mrs. Nelson's sixth-graders, working in small groups, have just finished a book study. Each group reads a different novel, and Mrs. Nelson has planned stations for the groups to complete together for their book. She has set up these five stations around the room:

Theme Station

INSTRUCTIONS: Use the supplies at the table to make a mini-poster that displays the theme of your book.

MATERIALS: Glue, scissors, paper, magazines, other crafting supplies.

Plot Sequencing Station

INSTRUCTIONS: Identify the most important events in your book. List them in order, using the graphic organizer.

MATERIALS: Graphic organizer, pencils.

Figurative Language Station

INSTRUCTIONS: Together with your team, find and categorize as many examples of figurative language in your book as you can.

MATERIALS: Paper, pencils.

Inferring Station

INSTRUCTIONS: Using a shared Google Doc, begin rewriting the book with one major plot twist. Make sure you include how this plot twist changes the events of the book.

MATERIALS: Devices.

Argument Station

INSTRUCTIONS: As a group, record a video in which you describe whether you would recommend this book to a classmate and why or why not.

MATERIALS: Recording-capable device.

Mrs. Nelson describes each station briefly to her class, emphasizing how students are to work together to complete each station's task. She assigns each group a starting station and explains they will have twenty-five minutes to complete each station. Then she dismisses students to begin working.

GROUP PROJECT

The famous (or infamous) group project can be used effectively in student-centered learning. Students are grouped, either by themselves or by the teacher, to complete a multi-step project. To ensure well-rounded groups, roles or tasks are distributed among members.

TIME: 30 to 60 minutes a day (may last several class sessions)

POSSIBLE MATERIALS: Expectations or instructions, rubric, research materials, work materials, role cards

COMMON APPLICATIONS: Application of mathematical processes, social studies research or simulations, scientific investigation, reading analysis, general research skills, special content areas

Role Cards Example

MANAGER	SPEAKER
Your role in the group:	*Your role in the group:*
• Keep everyone on-task • Make sure everyone knows their duties • Ask questions	• Present information to the class from the group • Read instructions and other materials
RECORDER	COACH
Your role in the group:	*Your role in the group:*
• Listen to group members' ideas • Write down important information and plans	• Encourage and provide assistance to other group members • Make sure everyone in the group is heard

Step-by-Step Guide

1. Divide the class into groups of two to six students.

2. Provide role cards or a list of roles. Have each student choose their own role or assign each student a role.

3. Present the expectations of the project and provide examples. Specify product options for the presentation of objectives.

   - This may be the time you also present the rubric if it has already been created.

4. Explain the duties of each assigned role.

5. Present key materials or resources and how to gain access to them.

6. Give students time and support to complete the described objectives.

   - If the project is going to take place over several days, you may provide additional explanations or reminders at the beginning of each work time.

7. Allow students to present their work, celebrate their work, or do both once the project is complete.

Teacher Prompts

- What can you accomplish to support your team?

- How does what you're doing right now help accomplish your team's goals?

- Are you fulfilling the duties of your role?

- How do you think this fits into your team's project?

- What resources might you need to make this happen?

VARIATIONS

- Start the group project as individual projects, and then have students work together to combine their projects into one project.

- Instead of presenting all the group project objectives at once, present one objective or aspect of the project per work session. Students work during a session to accomplish that objective.

Classroom Case Example

Mr. Lucas has been introducing students to economic principles, and now he wants students to experience them firsthand. Each student is grouped with two or three other students to work on the project, and each student is assigned a role. Mr. Lucas groups students and assigns roles based on a student preference survey. Once students learn their roles within their groups, Mr. Lucas explains the group project target. He is asking students to create a store where they sell one good or service. Students are to start with a given amount of funds, and they use some of the funds to buy materials and advertising, create the product, and sell the product to try to turn a profit. Mr. Lucas gives a couple of examples of goods and services that can be a final product, and he discusses budget tracking. He also reviews the scoring rubric.

Next, Mr. Lucas describes the duty of each assigned role. He asks students to sign a contract with their team to agree to fulfill their duties and work effectively with their "business partners." Mr. Lucas then presents the class with the materials and resources they will have access to while completing the project. He explains how he will help students stay on track. Students spend several class sessions working on the project before having a "shopping day," when students can buy goods or services. This day is followed by a wrap-up and reflection day.

ESCAPE ROOM OR BREAKOUT

In escape room or breakout activities, students work together at either the small-group or classwide level to solve a series of problems or puzzles, which leads to an "escape" or a "breakout." These activities are time-consuming, both to put together and to complete. But the resulting engagement and growth mindset are worth the time spent on them. These tasks can be set up virtually or in person.

TIME: 45 to 90 minutes

POSSIBLE MATERIALS: Lockbox, task materials, theme props

COMMON APPLICATIONS: Mathematical problem-solving, literary elements, science and technology problem-solving, any subject problem-solving

Step-by-Step Guide

1. Set a purpose for the activity and create a story that incorporates that purpose.

2. Create puzzles that accompany the story and clues to solve them.

   - Many resources can be purchased that will provide the story, puzzles, and clues for you.

3. Set up the materials, such as a lockbox, task cards, and props.

4. Rehearse for yourself what steps students will need to take in order to "escape" or "break out."

5. Introduce the activity to the class.

- The more enthusiasm you show when you present this activity, the more fun it will be for your students.

6. Explain the necessary elements of the process and the expectations for how the activity will be completed.

7. Set the time limit or reward.

- You may choose either to split the class into groups or to complete the tasks as a class. If you are splitting the class into groups, you may want to make it a competition rather than set a time limit.

8. Allow students to collaborate and problem-solve. Provide support but let students lead the activity.

9. Give students a chance to debrief, reflect, and celebrate.

Teacher Prompts

- Maybe there's another way to go about this.
- Did you hear what this student had to say?
- This reminds me of _____, which we've seen before.
- If that didn't work, what does that tell us?
- Way to problem-solve!

VARIATIONS

- Reverse the escape room experience by having students or groups of students create puzzles for their classmates to solve.
- Instead of setting up the puzzles and clues as an escape room, make it a scavenger hunt around the school building.

Classroom Case Example

Miss Walker's class is reviewing for an upcoming math assessment. She has created several puzzles involving word problems and skills from the current math unit. To organize her escape room, she has grouped students and given each group of students five clue envelopes and a box with five locks. Inside the box are plastic gold tokens, the "treasure."

Miss Walker sets the scene for the class by reading a short story describing how they will go on a treasure hunt. Each group must solve several puzzles to unlock their hidden treasure. To make things even more fun, Miss Walker has displayed an image of a pirate on a screen and is playing sea chanteys in the background. She goes over her expectations for the time. She also points out how collaboration should look for each group and that students should not give away answers to other groups. Then she dismisses the groups to begin their breakout journey. Along the way, she provides hints if necessary and manages the chaos.

Once every group has succeeded in opening their treasure box, Miss Walker reviews the most common issues or mistakes she noticed. Students reflect on the entire process, as well as the mathematical principles they employed.

PEER CONFERRING

In peer conferring, each student meets one-on-one with another student to receive feedback on their work. Peer conferring, which can take multiple structures, is centered around accomplishing one clear goal or learning target.

TIME: 5 to 15 minutes per conference

POSSIBLE MATERIALS: Peer feedback sheet, peer editing sheet, student works in progress, list of possible or common observations

COMMON APPLICATIONS: Individual projects, writing, mathematical problem-solving, reading strategies or response

Peer Feedback Sheet Example

PAIR PEER CONFERENCING	
Partner	What's your partner's name?
Admire	What do you admire about their work? 1. 2. 3.
Inquire	What do you want to ask about their work? 1. 2. 3.
Request	What would you request they change or add to their work? 1. 2. 3.

Step-by-Step Guide

1. Pair up students or allow students to choose a partner.

2. Model a peer conference for them in which partners present their work to each other and receive feedback from each other.

3. Provide time and space for students to pair up and present their work to each other.

4. Allow students to use the peer feedback sheet, peer editing sheet, or a list of possible or common conversations to provide feedback.

5. Give students the opportunity to adjust their work using the feedback they received.

6. Repeat the process so students can receive feedback from multiple students via conferences.

Teacher Prompts

- Someone else might notice something we don't.

- Take what they suggest and test it out.

- Give your partner clear examples of what you noticed.

- What can you tell your partner that will inspire them?

- What do you love about what they did?
- What are you going to take away and use in your own work?

Classroom Case Example

Students in Mr. Hall's music class have been writing song parodies. Many students are about to finish their first draft of their musical piece. Once students finish this draft, Mr. Hall wants them to meet in pairs to receive feedback on their songs.

Mr. Hall explains that on the front whiteboard is a grid for students to write their names when they are ready for a peer conference. Next to this area is a bin with peer feedback sheets. "If I am ready for a peer conference," Mr. Hall states, "I will go up to the board and put my name in the next empty box. The person whose name ends up next to mine is my partner for my first conference. I am not going to wait for my best friend. I am going to just put my name up in the next available space." Mr. Hall tells students that they will each grab a peer feedback sheet and then find a spot to meet with their partner.

Mr. Hall uses a student volunteer to help him demonstrate how a peer conference would look, as well as how to fill out the peer feedback sheet. He also demonstrates how he would receive feedback and use it to make changes to his work. Then he dismisses the students, who will continue working on their parodies and then confer with a peer when they finish their draft.

QUICK SHARE

A quick share occurs during a lesson or a break in independent work. In a quick share, students have a brief structured discussion with a partner or in a small group to further their understanding and discuss challenges.

TIME: 1 to 3 minutes

POSSIBLE MATERIALS: Student workspace materials (that is, personal whiteboards, paper, online document)

COMMON APPLICATIONS: During any content area lesson, after any content area guided or independent practice

Step-by-Step Guide

1. Present a prompt or question that gets to the heart of the learning target.

2. Give students time to think about the prompt.

3. Pair up or group students quickly.

   - It is helpful to have regular, predetermined partners or groups.

4. Set guidelines for the order of sharing as well as what the sharing should include.

   - Usually, these guidelines need to be discussed thoroughly only the first couple of times a quick share is employed.

5. Allow time for the first student in each pair or group to share their thoughts or answer to the prompt.

6. Ask students to switch and have the next student share their thoughts.

7. Repeat until each student in a pair or small group has shared at least once.

8. Give a few students the chance to tell the whole class what was discussed in their quick share.

Teacher Prompts

- I'm going to give you a chance to think about your answer first.

- Listen carefully to what your partner has to say.

- How can you build on what your partner had to say?

- Do you and your partner agree?

- How do you and your partner think about this differently?

Classroom Case Example

Miss Ivy is teaching a lesson about *Brown vs. Board of Education*. She began by showing a video explaining the court case and its outcome. She wants to ensure that her students have been processing the video before she moves on with more information and a class discussion. She asks students to think about the question: Why was the case *Brown vs. Board of Education* important? After giving them a minute to think, Miss Ivy asks each student to pair up with their predetermined partner, sitting beside them. She then says that she wants them to share with their partner the reasons the court case was important. She tells students that the person with the longer hair should share first. Students should put their hands in their lap once they are finished sharing. Once most of the students have their hands in their lap, she tells partners to switch roles.

After everyone has had a chance to share with their partner, Miss Ivy calls on a couple of students to share their thoughts until all the major points have been covered. This allows her to see how deeply students are conceptualizing the content, and what gaps need to be filled before moving on.

BARRIER GAME

Barrier games are an engaging way of exploring a concept. Students are partnered up and each student in a pair is given a different resource. While their partner remains blind to the resource, they must teach or convey the content from their resource to create a more complete picture of the concept for the other student.

TIME: 10 to 25 minutes

POSSIBLE MATERIALS: Review resources, task cards, student workspace materials (that is, personal whiteboards, paper, online document)

COMMON APPLICATIONS: Social-emotional learning, problem description, literary element identification, any content area review

Step-by-Step Guide

1. Create scenarios, problems, clues, vocabulary, or other task cards or materials that can be used to quiz or challenge students.

2. Pair up students.

3. Place a barrier between each pair so they cannot see each other's cards or materials.

   - Common barriers include folders, books, and devices. Or you can have students sit facing away from each other.

4. Tell students how to present a task to their partner and the goal of each task.

5. Have one student verbally present their cards first, while the other student tries to complete the task with the information they are given.

6. Allow students to remove the barrier to check their work when they believe they are done.

7. Have students switch roles and repeat the process.

8. Provide time for students to reflect on the experience and what they have learned.

Teacher Prompts

- What can you tell your partner that might help them?

- What can you ask your partner that might help you?

- Be as specific as you can to help your partner.

- Where do you think your partner made a mistake, and how can you help them correct it?

VARIATIONS

- Give both students in each pair the same cards, and have them discuss or work through the cards together without seeing each other's work.

- Add to the challenge by allowing only the partner presenting a task to talk, while the other partner remains silent.

Classroom Case Example

Ms. Ramsey is about to start teaching coding to her technology class. She wants students to understand how important it is for them to give clear instructions when coding. She has created two different silly drawings of faces. Around the room, there are pairs of students seated across from each other. Between each pair is a folder.

Ms. Ramsey introduces the challenge for the day. "I am going to give one partner a drawing and the other partner a blank page. The partner with the drawing will have to describe with as much detail as possible how to draw the picture they see in front of them. Their partner cannot see the drawing, so the first student should walk their partner through this step-by-step. The other student, who is drawing, cannot speak but must try their best to draw the picture as it is described."

Ms. Ramsey then hands out the pages, making sure that the second partner cannot see the already completed drawing. Once students have had time to work through the drawing process, Ms. Ramsey has them compare the original drawing with the one just drawn. Partners switch roles and repeat the process with a new example picture. At the end, Ms. Ramsey asks students to reflect on their experience. She connects the experience to how important it is to be detailed when coding.

STEM CHALLENGE

A STEM challenge is a collaborative project in which students embark on a process of exploration and design. Students are given an end goal, a challenge, or a problem and asked to design something to address it.

TIME: 25 to 200 minutes (may last several class sessions)

POSSIBLE MATERIALS: Design materials (paper and pencil, computer program), creation or building materials

COMMON APPLICATIONS: Scientific exploration and investigation, mathematical problem-solving

Step-by-Step Guide

1. Determine the end goal, challenge, or problem for students to address through design. For example, How tall can you build a tower of toothpicks?

2. Collect and organize materials.

3. Present students with the challenge and how to go about the design process.

4. Group students and have them meet to begin the brainstorming and design process.

5. Give students materials to test their designs.

6. Ask students to record or reflect on their results (or both) as they make changes to better their design.

7. Do a final test of completed designs as a whole group for a celebration or competition.

Teacher Prompts

- What could you design to make this happen?

- What are the flaws in the design? How can you address them?

- Did you listen to all the ideas presented in your group?

- What could you change to make your design even better?

- How does this design meet the challenge?

- Explain your thinking behind this design.

- Make a change and test it again.

- How did you put your ideas together to design a better solution?

VARIATIONS

- Make the challenge an independent project instead of a group one.

- Present students with an already created design, and ask them to improve upon it or create something more effective.

Classroom Case Example

Mrs. McLain has created a STEM challenge for her students: build a bridge of blocks that can hold a can of soup. She introduces the challenge to the class, sets out clear parameters, and groups students in threes. Then she hands out blueprint paper for students to sketch their designs. Each group is working on a design, and once they have a design they would like to create, they begin using the blocks to make it.

When a group signals to Mrs. McLain that they're done, she visits the group and places a can of soup on their bridge. If it falls she says, "How can you improve your design so it can support more weight?" If the can does not fall, she says the same thing, but she clarifies that next time they will test it with two cans. The design process of explore, design, and test is repeated until Mrs. McLain sees that every group has found a way to support at least one can of soup.

She wraps up the challenge by engaging students in a reflective discussion. She asks them which of their designs was the best and what made it so. Students also discuss their failures and how they adjusted their designs based on these failures.

Tips for Success: Ideas and Tools for Ensuring Collaboration Runs Smoothly

INTRODUCE "I FEEL" STATEMENTS. Collaborative learning inevitably leads to disagreements and hurt feelings. Students need to be able to address these situations, both in class and in real life. Prior to or during collaborative learning, introduce students to "I feel" statements. Teaching students to appropriately convey how they feel in a group can allow them to be great advocates for themselves. And teaching students how to listen and respond to others' statements is equally important. If students can listen to how someone feels and react with empathy and understanding, their collaborative learning experiences will be much more positive. If you get involved in resolving a group issue, starting with "I feel" statements can help students learn to problem-solve for themselves.

DISPLAY DUTIES. Everyone has duties in collaborative learning, even if everyone's duties are all the same. Displaying duties, or having them readily accessible to students via another means, helps students keep each other accountable. It also can make students feel more comfortable working in collaboration with others, as they know exactly what is expected of them during the activity.

ADAPT ACTIVITIES. Some collaborative activities may not work as well for some classes or some teachers as others. Adjust an activity as you see fit, even if it has already begun. For example, if you have asked students to record large amounts of information by typing, but you realize they are taking too much time to get ideas down rather than truly absorbing the information, adjust your approach. Ask students instead to research and then video record as a group what they have learned.

PROVIDE SPACE. Make sure the layout of the classroom during collaborative learning lends itself to the size of the groups that students will be working in and the tasks they will complete. Spacing groups out as much as possible allows students to feel more comfortable in their working environment and helps keep the volume of student voices to a reasonable level.

PAUSE AND POINT OUT. Collaborative learning is largely about allowing students to problem-solve and learn with other students. But if you circulate throughout the room and observe many groups are struggling with the issue, pause the whole class and help them get back on the right track.

THINK ABOUT LANGUAGE. When students are working together, think about what language you use to describe student groups and actions. For example, referring to groups as *teams* or *partners* can highlight the fact that group members rely on one another. Using verbiage such as *collaborate*, *communicate*, *mentor*, and *present* can help students recognize the meanings of these words and apply the skills they learn to other aspects of their lives.

PROMOTE INCLUSIVITY. When you notice that some students are struggling to participate in the group setting, teach students tools and phrases to include others, as well as participate. This can be as simple as, What do you think? or Can I add something here? Teaching students to see, hear, and generally include one another is an important life skill and fits in perfectly with collaborative learning.

START SMALL. Get students comfortable with working in a group by putting them with a well-matched pair or small group. Having more than two or three students in a group can sometimes lead to voices being drowned out, especially those of quieter students. Sometimes even breaking a larger group into smaller working pairs can help. Start with smaller groups, and once you see students successfully working in this kind of collaborative setting, you might want to increase group size in the future.

CHAPTER 5

INDEPENDENT EXPLORATION ACTIVITIES

Independent exploration activities allow students to take all the tools they have acquired and strategies they have learned and apply them. These activities also allow students to reflect on their own learning. These benefits feed into the larger benefit of students finding meaning in their learning. When students know that what they are doing in school has a purpose and is useful in their lives, their educational experience is much more successful.

Independent exploration is important for teachers to employ before giving students summative assessments because it allows students to find their gaps in understanding.

SELF-ASSESSMENT OF GOAL PROGRESS

This self-assessment activity allows students to use one of a variety of reflection or scoring tools to monitor how they are progressing toward their overall goals or targets. It pairs well with student goal-setting conferences or check-in conferences.

TIME: 2 to 10 minutes

POSSIBLE MATERIALS: Goal record sheet (see page 52), star and steps (see page 55) or other self-assessment, reflection prompts

COMMON APPLICATIONS: Any content area with measurable growth, mathematical problem-solving goals, reading strategy application or skill goals, writing strategy application or skill goals, social-emotional goals

Step-by-Step Guide

1. Ask students to find or remind themselves of their personal goal for a specific area.

2. Give students a method of self-assessment and the materials for it.

3. Model the self-assessment process.

4. Allow students time to reflect on their progress toward their goal.

5. Ask them to complete the self-assessment task you have given them or allow them to pick from a few self-assessment options.

Teacher Prompts

- Think about where you started with this goal and where you are now.

- What have you already done to achieve your goal?

- Is there anything you need from me to help you continue making progress toward your goal?

- What do you still need to do to achieve your goal?

- Was this goal a good fit for you?

- What are your next steps?

- Think about how you feel about the goal.

- What does it take to master this goal?

VARIATIONS

- Instead of prompting all students to self-assess at the same time, set up a system or schedule for regular self-assessment. This may even be part of the initial goal-setting. For example, if students have a reading goal, they could plan to assess after every chapter they finish in a book.

- Pair with a check-in conference.

Classroom Case Example

Mrs. Evans asks students to look at their personal goal they have stuck to the outside of their storage cubby. In her special education classroom, each of Mrs. Evans's students has a goal that can apply to work in any subject area. Mrs. Evans asks students to grab their goal and bring it to a work table.

Next, Mrs. Evans has each student read their goal out loud and explain what it means. Then she shows students star and steps, a self-assessment tool. She walks the class through this self-assessment with her own goal of being patient with herself when she doesn't understand something. Mrs. Evans explains that she has mastered the skill of staying calm when she is puzzled. She points out that her next steps are to use positive self-talk when she gets to something challenging.

Mrs. Evans asks her students to think about where they are with their own goal. She has them discuss this briefly with her before allowing them to fill out their self-assessment.

SELF-ASSESSMENT OF UNDERSTANDING

In this self-assessment activity, students are given a means by which to reflect on and convey how well they understand the content at hand. They also determine the areas where they need help to understand the content.

TIME: 1 to 5 minutes

POSSIBLE MATERIALS: Student workspace materials (that is, personal whiteboards, paper, online document), self-assessment of understanding form or anchor chart (that is, thumbs up, middle, or down; or stoplight)

COMMON APPLICATIONS: Any content area formative or summative assessment, any content area instruction

Thumbs Up, Middle, or Down Anchor Chart Example

I get it!	I kinda get it!	I don't get it yet.
I understand everything!	I need a little help.	I need a lot of help.

I can tell you what I learned.	I still have a few questions.	I still have a lot of questions.

Stoplight Anchor Chart Example

TRAFFIC LIGHT ASSESSMENT	
	I need some help understanding!
	I think I understand, but I may need a little help.
	I understand! I can do it by myself.

Step-by-Step Guide

1. Remind students of the learning target at hand.

2. Give students a method of self-assessment and the materials for it.

3. Model the self-assessment process.

4. Allow students time to reflect on their understanding of the specific learning target.

5. Ask them to complete the self-assessment.

Teacher Prompts

- Where are you with this learning target?

- How well do you understand what I am asking you to do?

- Tell me how much this makes sense to you right now.

- How much more practice and help do you think you need to understand this fully?

- Where are your gaps in understanding?

VARIATIONS

- Have students complete an assignment or a task that helps them achieve the learning target. Then have students submit their work to you in a designated spot, which allows them to self-assess how they felt about their understanding of the target during the task. For example, you could have a green, a yellow, and a red bin for three levels of understanding.

- Add a self-assessment activity to the bottom of a practice piece so students can self-assess their understanding of what they have just done.

Classroom Case Example

Ms. Reynolds's students have been studying a strategy called adding on to subtract. They are learning to subtract within 100. She has been doing guided practice with her students and wants to give students a problem to try on their own. Before giving students the problem, she points out that to the side of the problem is a stoplight image. She demonstrates the thought process behind choosing a stoplight color to circle.

"If after solving the problem, you feel you completely understood it, circle the green light. If you feel you mostly understand, but could use some more help, circle the yellow light. If you feel you don't really understand and need help, circle the red light." After this explanation, Ms. Reynolds hands out the problem. Students are to solve the problem and then self-assess their work.

SELF-ASSESSMENT OF PERFORMANCE

For this activity, students use the scoring rubric for an assignment or assessment to score their own performance. Using their self-scoring, they make improvements to their work before submitting or presenting it.

TIME: 5 to 20 minutes

POSSIBLE MATERIALS: Rubric or scoring criteria, student works in progress (that is, assignment or project, assessment)

COMMON APPLICATIONS: Any content area projects, any content area written explanations or pieces, any content area performance tasks

Step-by-Step Guide

1. Review rubric criteria and their meaning

2. Provide every student with a rubric.

3. Instruct students that once they are close to completing their assignment or assessment, they should revisit the rubric to score themselves on each criterion.

4. Briefly model for students what the process for self-assessment and the corrections that follow should look like.

5. Ensure that students have time to self-assess their work and make any corrections before they submit their work.

Teacher Prompts

- How do you rate your work as it is now?

- How can you make sure you meet all the criteria?

- What areas have you mastered?

- In what areas can you make a few more improvements?

- Would you be proud to submit or present this work?

VARIATION

- Before final scoring, you can score students' work for them. They can compare this score with their self-assessment. They can also use this score to put the final touches on their work.

Classroom Case Example

Mr. Robinson's students are working on an ancient civilizations project. Mr. Robinson begins the class session by displaying the project's rubric. He reviews the key criteria from the rubric with the class. Then he hands out another copy of the rubric to the students. As the class is listening, Mr.

Robinson uses the displayed rubric to model how to self-assess each criterion, one at a time, using the project. He tells students that when they think their project is almost finished, they should use the rubric to self-assess. Once they self-assess, they should make any necessary changes so that they will get their best possible score.

CHOICE MENUS OR BOARDS

A choice menu or board allows students freedom of choice while they still make progress toward the same learning target. The teacher provides an organizer in which different tasks are listed. Each student is given an outline of what they must complete from the organizer, but they choose which tasks to do to meet this expectation.

TIME: 40 to 150 minutes (may last several class sessions)

POSSIBLE MATERIALS: Choice menu, choice board, materials for each choice

COMMON APPLICATIONS: Rehearsal of any content skill set

Choice Menu Example

CHOICE MENU			
Choose one item from each section to complete.			
Appetizers	*Entrees*	*Sides*	*Desserts*
Item 1	Item 1	Item 1	Item 1
Item 2	Item 2	Item 2	Item 2
Item 3	Item 3	Item 3	Item 3
Item 4	Item 4	Item 4	Item 4

Choice Board Example

CHOICE BOARD				
Choose five activities from the board below to complete.				
Option A	Option B	Option C	Option D	Option E
Option F	Option G	Option H	Option I	Option J
Option K	Option L	Option M	Option N	Option O
Option P	Option Q	Option R	Option S	Option T
Option U	Option V	Option W	Option X	Option Y

Step-by-Step Guide

1. Create a choice menu or board that includes engaging tasks for the intended content.

   - Aim for each task to take about the same amount of time to complete.

2. Remind students of the learning target.

3. Introduce students to the menu or board by explaining the options it includes and stating your expectations for how many tasks are to be completed.

4. Give students time and materials to complete the tasks.

   - Have students complete additional tasks if they complete the minimum requirement.

Teacher Prompts

- Which of the options are you most interested in completing?
- Which of the choices do you think you'll get the most out of?
- How can you challenge yourself today?
- How can you enjoy learning today?
- What choices can I clarify for you?

Classroom Case Example

Ms. Palma wants her students to practice their math fluency in all four operations. She creates a choice menu for students to practice their math fluency skills, and she creates a ten-minute time slot in the daily schedule for students to work on their menu. Ms. Palma then introduces the menu to her class and explains each of the activity options as well as how to go about completing the menu. Students are then given the time to work on the menu over the course of several class sessions. If students finish the menu early, Ms. Palma asks them to pick another item from the menu to complete.

MUNCHY MATH MENU

Choose one item from each section to complete. Highlight each item you choose.

Appetizers	Entrees	Sides	Desserts
Watch three of the multiplication song videos.	Complete the subtraction puzzle.	Play the addition game from our online classroom for 15 minutes.	Create a poster to demonstrate your favorite division strategy.
Complete the multiplication color by number.	Play the dice-rolling subtraction game for six rounds.	Solve the odd problems from the addition practice sheet.	Make a video to explain what division is.
Play the multiplication game from our online classroom for 15 minutes.	Write three subtraction word problems and create an answer key for them.	Play the addition card game for 10 minutes.	Create a model of a division problem and take a picture of it with the matching equation.

INDEPENDENT PROJECT

Students are given an independent project prompt, taught the skills needed to complete that prompt, and shown examples of completed independent projects. Students should have choice and support throughout their time completing the project, which ultimately should be a presentable finished product.

TIME: 30 to 60 minutes per day (may last several class sessions)

POSSIBLE MATERIALS: Expectations or instructions, rubric, research materials, work materials

COMMON APPLICATIONS: Application of mathematical processes, social studies research or simulations, scientific investigation, reading analysis, general research skills, special content areas

Step-by-Step Guide

1. Present the objectives of the project and provide examples. Specify product options for the presentation of objectives.

   - This may be the time you also present the rubric if it has already been created.

2. Explain the expectations or instructions for independent work time.

3. Present materials or resources and how to gain access to them.

4. Give students time and support to complete the described objectives.

   - If the project is going to take place over several days, you may provide additional explanations or reminders at the beginning of each work time.

5. Allow students to present or celebrate their work (or both) once the project is complete.

Teacher Prompts

- What direction will you be taking this project?

- How do you think this will meet the criteria?

- What will your final product include?

- What support do you need?

- What is your plan for making this happen?

- How have you had to adjust your project plans?

- What are your next steps?

- How can you use your time efficiently?

Classroom Case Example

Mrs. Franklin is starting a "genius hour" project with her students. For this project, students can explore any phenomenon or learn about any concept they are passionate about. They must research their topic and create a final product that demonstrates application of their learning. Due to the open-ended nature of the project, Mrs. Franklin has created a rubric that lists what students must include in their genius hour project. The rubric includes items such as, "The student is an expert on the topic" and "The topic is unique." Mrs. Franklin reviews the rubric with her students and provides a few examples of past students' work.

Then Mrs. Franklin outlines the project's process and how class time is to be used to complete this process. She also points out resources students may use for research and tools they may use to create their final product. Each class session that students are working on the project, Mrs. Franklin addresses the entire class with possible next steps, provides an updated timeline, and meets with individual students to provide guidance. Once students have completed the project, they present their final product to the class and celebrate all they have accomplished.

MINI-LESSON PRACTICE

Mini-lesson practice accompanies a whole-group or small-group model mini-lesson. In this activity, fluid or more organized tasks are given to students. They are told their goal for these tasks is to try out on their own the skills or strategies presented in a mini-lesson.

TIME: 5 to 30 minutes

POSSIBLE MATERIALS: Sticky notes, notebook, practice page, student workspace materials (that is, personal whiteboards, paper, online document)

COMMON APPLICATIONS: Mathematics, reading comprehension and analysis, writing process and skills

Step-by-Step Guide

1. Teach a model mini-lesson.

2. Assign or present a task that allows students to practice applying the skill taught in the mini-lesson.

3. Give students time to complete the task.

4. Ask students to share or collect evidence of student practice.

Teacher Prompts

- How can you connect this to what you learned in the mini-lesson?

- If you need to refresh your memory, look at the anchor chart.

- Can you show me how to apply this to your own _____?

- What an excellent example of _____!

- How can we use this in other situations?

VARIATIONS

- Have the mini-lesson practice within a few days following a model mini-lesson to help students maintain what they have learned.

- Allow students the option of working with a partner to practice collaborative learning and communication skills.

Classroom Case Example

Mr. Thompson has taught a model mini-lesson about using dialogue in writing. He tells students that today, while they are working in their writing journal, he would like for them to challenge themselves to add dialogue to their writing. He gives students twenty minutes to work on their writing. Then Mr. Thompson has students share with a partner where they included dialogue in their writing.

Tips for Success: Ideas for How to Keep Students Focused, Accountable, and Productive During Independent Exploration

JOURNAL REFLECTIONS. A great way to house self-assessments and maintain accountability for independent exploration is a journal. If you do not have other evidence of completion of a task or do not want to have to collect this evidence from students, a short journal reflection can provide you with a picture of where students are at with the content at hand. Journal writing is also a great way for students to practice their written explanations and reflection skills.

CREATING A SYSTEM FOR ASSISTANCE. Plan out how you want students to ask for help during independent exploration. Otherwise, you will have students approaching you wherever you are in the room. If you plan on meeting with small groups or conferring while other students are working independently, you may want to assign specific students the job of helping answer their classmates' questions.

ADAPT FOR INDIVIDUALS. The beauty of independent work is that you can personalize it. If you think some students need more of a challenge, or some students need less volume of work, then you can make either happen with simple adjustments. Make these adjustments private between you and each student, and discuss why you would like to make the adjustments with the student. This way, every student knows that they are being held to their own set of high expectations.

ACCOUNT FOR AMBIENCE. Especially when students are being asked to work or explore independently, be aware of what each student needs their atmosphere to be. Some students cannot work well in silence. Other students prefer silence to limit distractions. Some students need to be sitting up at a desk or table, while others like to lay out their supplies around them on the floor. If possible, look to accommodate all preferences for independent work. A good solution for sound may be playing soft instrumental music or white noise in the background. It may even be an option for students to play soft sound through headphones. Providing different seating options might also help students focus.

CHAPTER 6

TEACHER–STUDENT RELATIONSHIP-BUILDING ACTIVITIES

Relationships have been proven to be a key element of what makes student-centered learning effective. Arguably, the most important relationship in the classroom is between student and teacher. For many teachers, including myself, our relationship with our students is our favorite aspect of teaching. It is why we get up and go to work each day. But especially if our relationships with our students are healthy and productive, we might not include much time for building teacher–student relationships past the beginning of the school year. Relationships need nurturing. If we get too caught up in day-to-day activities and the academic achievements of our students, we can lose sight of the personal relationship with students that helps them be comfortable and succeed. The activities in this chapter are quick ways we can build our relationships with individual students.

EMOTIONAL CHECK-IN

An emotional check-in can take place in many different ways. This activity lets students express where they are at emotionally, say why that is where they are at, and ask for adult assistance if they want help coping with their emotions. The check-in allows students to feel heard by their teacher and learn to be vulnerable with trusted adults.

TIME: 5 minutes

POSSIBLE MATERIALS: Check-in sheet, zones or emotions chart

COMMON APPLICATIONS: Beginning of the day, midday, after an event or after returning from another classroom, end of the day

Emotions Chart Example

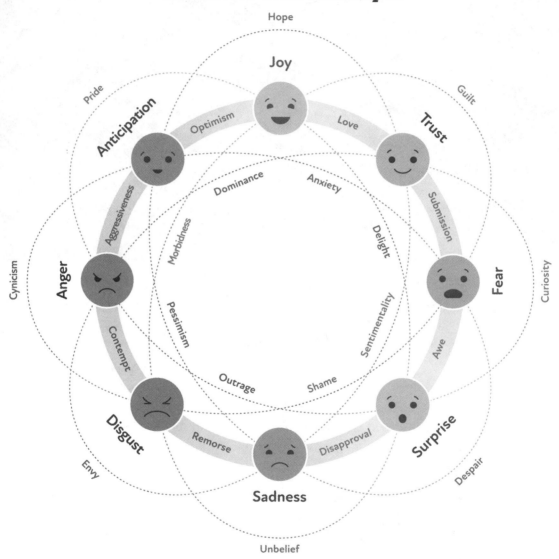

CLASSROOM-READY RESOURCES FOR STUDENT-CENTERED LEARNING

Step-by-Step Guide

1. Determine the medium by which you will be checking in with your students.

2. Give every student the chance to complete the check-in.

3. Provide opportunities for students to share how they are feeling, why they are feeling this way, and what you can do to help them.

   • All the information within the check-in process should be given voluntarily.

4. Follow up with students who would like help dealing with difficult emotions.

Teacher Prompts

• What emotion are you experiencing right now?

• What can I do to support you?

• How can you get ready to learn?

• Would you like to share with me the reasons you feel this way?

• What tools do you need to help you cope with your emotions?

VARIATIONS

• Expand the check-in beyond emotions so that students can share with you anything that is going on in their lives, even if it is not currently distressing them.

• Allow students to simply move a magnet, sticky note, or another item to an area designated for certain emotions. Then have students who are identifying emotions that could inhibit their learning follow up with explanations if they wish.

Classroom Case Example

When students enter Mr. Dillard's classroom, they have a check-in sheet sitting on their desks. Students are instructed by Mr. Dillard to fill out the page with as much information as they would like and return it to him. As Mr. Dillard receives the pages, he reads them and keeps track of where students are at, particularly if they are not doing well or are requesting a check-in with him. Mr. Dillard records this information so he can meet with these students once everyone is working independently.

JOURNAL PASS

Journal passing takes place for several days, several weeks, or even the entire year. In this activity the teacher and student share a journal. The journal is a means of communication for students who need extra attention or struggle to communicate otherwise.

TIME: 5 minutes per pass

POSSIBLE MATERIALS: Journal, notebook, or sketchbook

COMMON APPLICATIONS: Morning arrival, independent writing time, end of the day

Step-by-Step Guide

1. Determine what students would benefit most from a journal pass.

   - You may choose to do this with every student—but it is time-consuming.

2. Provide students with a journal, notebook, or sketchbook.

3. Meet with students to explain that the journal can be used for them to share with you any thoughts, feelings, or concerns they have via writing or drawing.

4. Explain to students what times it would be appropriate to write or draw in the journal and where to put it when they are ready for you to look at it and respond.

5. Tell students you will reply when you are able.

6. Specify that this will be seen by only you and them unless they share a concern for their safety, in which case you would have to share their journal with other trusted adults.

7. Start the journal pass either by giving students time to write or draw in it immediately or by writing a brief note in the journal and giving it to them to respond.

Teacher Prompts

- This will allow you to share with me without worrying that other students might hear your feelings if you do not wish them to.

- Write what you feel.

- Draw what you feel.

- Share with me how I can help you.

- What do you want me to know?

- Show me what I should know about you.

- Provide a mailbox in which any student can place a message to you throughout the day.

- Build journaling into your daily schedule and allow students to choose whether they journal to themselves or write to you.

Classroom Case Example

Ms. Lancaster has a student who has been difficult to connect with verbally. She notices the student is struggling to do her classwork but enjoys sketching on her papers. Ms. Lancaster wants to try a journal pass with this student. She calls the student over to meet with her and lets the student choose from a few options of colored notebooks.

"I'd like to start a journal with you," Ms. Lancaster explains. "This will be our journal. In it you can write or draw anything you would like me to know or see. I will respond to you in it as soon as I can. What you write will stay just between you and me unless you share with me something that puts you in danger. Then I would have to share that with another trusted adult."

She hands the notebook to the student, telling her, "Set it on my desk when you are ready for me to read it."

QUESTION OF THE DAY

Question of the day is a quick activity in which students are asked and able to answer a fun or interesting open-ended question. The goal of the question is for the teacher to get to know their students a little better and for students to be put at ease.

TIME: 5 minutes

POSSIBLE MATERIALS: Prompt book or list

COMMON APPLICATIONS: During transitions, social-emotional learning, or short brain break

Step-by-Step Guide

1. Generate an open-ended question that every student would enjoy or feel comfortable answering in front of the class.

   - You may wish to use a book or list to provide ideas for prompts.

2. Ask the question of the class.

3. Give each student an opportunity to answer the question if they wish.

4. Provide brief positive feedback to student responses.

Teacher Prompts

- Would you like to share your answer?
- What is your answer?
- I love that answer!
- Such a creative response!
- Thank you for sharing that!

VARIATIONS

- Allow a student to come up with the question of the day. Screen it before you ask it to the class.

- Have students write or draw their answer instead of responding out loud.

Classroom Case Example

Mr. Rivera's students are returning to the classroom from lunch. As they are lined up in the hallway outside the classroom, he asks students to think about their answer to the question, "What is the animal, other than a human, you are most like?" He gives students a little bit of time to think on the question and then prompts students to enter the classroom. As they enter the classroom, each student tells Mr. Rivera their answer to the question. Mr. Rivera gives quick responses as he hears each student's thoughts.

PERSONAL GREETING

The personal greeting is an activity in which students create a handshake, a dance, or another greeting to do with their teacher each day. Students have fun and feel special as the teacher meets them with their own unique greeting.

TIME: 20 seconds per student

POSSIBLE MATERIALS: Hand sanitizer

COMMON APPLICATIONS: Morning arrival, returning to the classroom, end of day

Step-by-Step Guide

1. Provide general guidelines for greeting options.

   - You may wish to clarify that you cannot touch hands in the greeting, or make sure you have hand sanitizer available.

2. Give an example.

3. Allow students to brainstorm and practice their greeting, possibly with a peer.

4. Have students practice their greeting with you.

5. Use the greeting with the student every day at the same time, for example, when students arrive at the classroom each morning.

Teacher Prompts

- How can you make your greeting special or unique?

- Make a greeting you will enjoy doing each day.

- How can you start or end the day with a smile?

- Let's practice this. I want to get it right.

VARIATIONS

- Allow students to pick a new greeting each day, one that you will copy.

- Have students come up with a phrase to say as a greeting, rather than a physical handshake or dance move combination.

Classroom Case Example

Mrs. Lewis is teaching students their morning procedures. She tells students that before entering her classroom, students must greet her. The greeting must be a handshake, dance, or a little of both, but it should be unique to them. Then Mrs. Lewis demonstrates a handshake that ends with a high five and a hug. She gives students time to create and practice their greetings, while she goes around the room to help students who are struggling to come up with ideas. Once everyone has their greeting and has had time to practice it, she has students enter the hallway and practice greeting her, one at a time. She reminds students that they are to greet her this way each morning, and she will eventually memorize each greeting.

END-OF-DAY EXIT SLIP

Rather than having students provide academic information on an exit slip, the end-of-day exit slip gives students an opportunity to reflect on their day and let their teacher know how it went. Students can convey how they felt about the day without being overheard or seen by other students. Teachers can get to know what students' daily experiences are like in their classroom.

TIME: 5 minutes

POSSIBLE MATERIALS: Exit slips or notecards

COMMON APPLICATIONS: End of class session or day

Exit Slips Example

END-OF-DAY EXIT SLIP
Name:
Circle the emoji that best summarizes how you feel about today:
Why did you circle that emoji?
What was your favorite part of today?
What was your least favorite part of your day?

Step-by-Step Guide

1. Hand out the exit slips or notecards.

2. Read or review the information you would like provided to you on the slip.

3. Give students time to complete the exit slip.

4. Provide the means for students to privately turn in the slip.

  • Ensure students have a quiet follow-up activity so that every student can take their time to finish.

5. Read over the exit slips to process the information, touch base with any students you need to, and plan any changes you need to make.

Teacher Prompts

• Please include anything I need to know about your day.

• Let me know how I can be the best teacher for you.

• Let me know what has been going well for you.

VARIATIONS

• Instead of doing a private exit slip, have students share aspects of their day in a whole-group setting.

• Make the exit slip part of a daily journaling exercise.

Classroom Case Example

It's almost the end of the school day, so Mr. Gilmore hands out his end-of-day exit slips. He reads each item on the exit slip aloud for students and then gives them time to complete it. Mr. Gilmore tells students to flip over the page when they are finished, so he knows he can come collect it. As he collects the pages, Mr. Gilmore quickly glances at the emojis students circled. If he finds any of them concerning, he makes a note to address this with the student during pack up. Otherwise, he saves the pages to reflect on after the school day has ended.

Tips for Success: How to Boost Teacher–Student Relationships

START FROM DAY ONE. Although teacher–student relationship-building activities can be added at any point in the school year, it's best to start regularly implementing them from day one. This way, students know they can count on you to check in with them, and you start getting to know your students right away.

RECOGNIZE WHO NEEDS IT MORE. Every student needs to establish a good relationship with their teacher. Some students may need more positive adult interactions in their lives or have a harder time opening up than others. These students are good candidates for regular journal passes or occasionally having lunch with you in the classroom.

TAKE THE STUDENT'S LEAD. Children are usually very good about unintentionally showing you how they best build relationships. Many students want to share their interests with you, some want to share their accomplishments, and others want to share their affection. Follow the student's lead to show your care in the ways they demonstrate they would best receive it.

CHAPTER 7

COMMUNITY-BUILDING ACTIVITIES

Creating a classroom, and furthermore a school community, that feels like family is a worthwhile goal. When your students have each other's back, they will treat each other with respect, learn from one another, and feel comfortable in their school environment. When students can be participatory members of a classroom community, they are more likely to participate in the community outside the classroom as well.

MORNING MEETING

Similar to a class meeting, a morning meeting allows students to touch base with each other first thing. It can set the tone and provide the structure for heading into the school day or school week. Although the teacher may lead the morning meeting, every student should have the opportunity to have their voice heard.

TIME: 5 to 15 minutes

POSSIBLE MATERIALS: Interactive or dance music

COMMON APPLICATIONS: Beginning of the day or the class session, beginning of the week

Step-by-Step Guide

1. Have students sit in a circle on the floor or at their desks. Make sure there is a spot for you as well.

2. Begin the meeting with a brief greeting or song.

3. Review the schedule or changes for the day or the week.

4. Allow students the opportunity to either ask questions or share something going into the day.

   - You may wish to provide a brief prompt, such as, What is one thing you did over the weekend?

5. Address any celebrations or concerns you want every student to be aware of for the day.

6. Wrap up the meeting with an encouraging class mantra, phrase, or cheer.

Teacher Prompts

- Today we will _____.
- This week will include _____.
- What questions do you have about _____?
- How will you make today successful?
- Show your classmates you are ready to listen.

VARIATIONS

- Instead of meeting at the beginning of the day or week, meet at the end of the day or week to reflect on what has gone on during that time, as well as what is coming up.

- Create a student job of leading the morning meeting so that a student addresses most major agenda items with the group.

Classroom Case Example

Mr. Cooley calls his kindergartners to the carpet at the beginning of their Monday school day. They calmly sit in a circle as they do for their morning meeting every morning. Mr. Cooley begins the meeting by saying, "Good morning, class!"

Students reply, "Good morning, Mr. Cooley." Then Mr. Cooley describes the class schedule for the day, including what special content area class they have that day. He allows students to ask any questions they have about the week. Next, he asks students to raise their hands if they would like to share one thing they did over the weekend. He clarifies that this is just one thing, so that everyone has the chance to share. Mr. Cooley takes the time to allow every student who would like to share to do so. He even shares one thing he did over the weekend.

Then Mr. Cooley reminds students of their class goal to transition efficiently and the rewards that come with achieving enough efficient transitions. He wraps up the class meeting by leading the class in their class cheer.

TEAM CREATION

In the activity of team creation, students placed in a seating or collaborative learning group create a team identity. This can include a team name, handshake, motto, symbol, flag, or even song. The creation of the team builds a sense of community between students before they begin working together on more academic tasks.

TIME: 5 to 20 minutes (tasks may take several class sessions)

POSSIBLE MATERIALS: Arts and crafts materials

COMMON APPLICATIONS: Formation of new seating arrangements or new groups, beginning a collaborative learning activity

Step-by-Step Guide

1. Have students meet in their newly formed groups.

2. Have students introduce themselves, and prompt them to provide a piece of information about themselves.

3. Give them one or more tasks to complete to begin forming their team identity.

   - Tasks may include creating a team name, handshake, motto, symbol, flag, or song.

4. Provide an example of the task, and possibly model or explain how the group may go about completing the task.

5. Have students present or demonstrate their team identity to you or the class.

6. Repeat for multiple class sessions with different elements of team identity if you wish.

Teacher Prompts

- How can you include everyone in this process?

- What would allow everyone in the group to be represented?

- Does everyone agree with this?

- Could you combine _____ with _____?

- What does your team stand for?

> ### VARIATIONS
>
> - Provide a specific system for how students will create a team identity. For example, every group member will write one word on a sticky note, and those words combined will be the team's name.
>
> - Allow teams to compete against each other in an easygoing manner as a classroom management technique.

Classroom Case Example

Ms. Wilkerson has just assigned her students new table seats. She wants her students to get to know and collaborate with their new tablemates. To begin this process she has students introduce themselves, even if they know each other, and share one "boring" fact about themselves. Once every group has had everyone share, she lets the groups know that each group will be creating a team name.

"Here are the rules," Ms. Wilkerson says. "Your team name must be appropriate, everyone in your group must agree on the name, and you should all compromise so that everyone has a little something they like in the name. Once your team has decided on its name, raise your hands."

Ms. Wilkerson gives the students time to work together to come up with their team name. When groups raise their hands, Ms. Wilkerson checks their name and hands them a poster paper to get started on their team flag to display their new name.

KINDNESS CHALLENGE

A kindness challenge can be used to build community in either your classroom or the entire school. In a kindness challenge, students receive a prompt to complete a specific act of kindness and are given the time and means to complete the activity within the school day.

TIME: 5 to 20 minutes

POSSIBLE MATERIALS: Arts and crafts or writing materials

COMMON APPLICATIONS: Social-emotional learning

Step-by-Step Guide

1. Generate an idea for a simple act of kindness, or brainstorm optional acts of kindness as a class.

   - Example acts include writing and decorating kind notes to a classmate or staff member, cleaning up areas of the school, or recording encouraging videos.

2. Describe the act of kindness and the guidelines for completing it.

3. Give students time to complete the act of kindness.

4. Ask students to reflect on the outcomes of their act of kindness.

Teacher Prompts

- What can you do to make someone's day better?

- What's something you might not normally do, but we can try today to show a little kindness?

- How can you make this person feel special or important?

- How can we make our classroom or world a better place?

VARIATIONS

- Carry out a kindness attack: students all do the same act of kindness for the same person.

- Give students a kindness challenge they can complete at home. The next day, they can share about how it went.

Classroom Case Example

While her students are gathered on the carpet, Mrs. Whitlow asks them, "Would you like to commit an awesome act of kindness today?" Students are intrigued. Mrs. Whitlow further explains to students what an act of kindness entails and helps them brainstorm a list of ideas. Then she has the class vote on the act of kindness they would like to complete today. The act with the most votes is writing positive notes to students' former teachers. They determine as a class that each note should include the teacher's name and at least one reason why this teacher is outstanding. Students are given time to write their notes.

Once students have written notes to one or more teachers, they deliver the notes by taping them to teachers' classroom doors. When students return to the classroom, Mrs. Whitlow moves onto other items on the day's agenda. As the day progresses, and students have heard from some of the teachers how much their notes meant, students take time to talk about the act of kindness and reflect on its impact on others and themselves.

TALK TIME

A structured talk time during the school day can allow students to get to know one another better, as well as practice their conversation skills. This activity can be used once or frequently to give students the chance to socialize with students in the classroom they otherwise might not visit with.

TIME: 5 to 15 minutes

POSSIBLE MATERIALS: Conversation or question cards or presentable slides

COMMON APPLICATIONS: Social-emotional learning

Conversation Cards Example

"*Whom do you admire and why?*"	"*What makes you unique?*"	"*What can you do if you don't feel good about something you see or hear?*"
"*What would you do if you were being bullied? If you saw someone else being bullied?*"	"*Which superhero would you like to be? Why?*"	"*Which three words best describe you?*"

Step-by-Step Guide

1. Group students or pair up students.

   • You may simply choose to group or pair up students who are already sitting near each other.

2. Model an example conversation with the tools you will be using.

3. Give students a set of conversation prompts or questions, or present students with one prompt at a time.

4. Allow students time to converse.

5. Circulate throughout the room, and make observations about what students are doing well and what could use improvement.

- Examples include listening, making eye contact, and not interrupting.

6. Provide feedback to students about what you noticed or give students time to share with the group something they learned about their partner.

Teacher Prompts

- How can you show your partner you are listening?

- What can you ask your partner to expand upon?

- How can you make sure your partner's voice is heard?

- What do you want to know about your partner?

- Can you connect with what your partner has said?

- Speak clearly and kindly.

VARIATIONS

- Incorporate talk time into a content area lesson by giving students talking prompts, both on topic and off topic.

- Have students move around the room so they are visiting with students outside one partnership or group.

- Have students create their own prompts or questions to discuss with their partners.

Classroom Case Example

Ms. Stanley's students are about to begin a new group project. Before they do so, Ms. Stanley wants students to become better acquainted with the other students in their group. She models for students how they will be using a set of question cards, taking turns sharing their answers to the question with the group. While modeling this, she emphasizes that students can respond to other people's answers but not interrupt them. She gives each group a stack of question cards and allows them to begin sharing.

While students are talking with one another, Ms. Stanley circulates throughout the room. She gives reminders to students when necessary and makes observations about group dynamics. Once students have had time to share, Ms. Stanley pauses the activity and asks a few students to share with the class one new thing they have learned about someone in their group.

SHOW AND TELL

The classic show and tell activity allows students to choose something important to them and share it with their classmates. It allows students to build relationships with one another while also promoting presentation and listening skills.

TIME: 5 to 10 minutes per student

POSSIBLE MATERIALS: Personal items

COMMON APPLICATIONS: Social-emotional learning, generation of writing ideas, exposure to different books or genres

Step-by-Step Guide

1. Determine the time frame for show and tell.

2. Inform students and parents when it will be their turn to bring in and share a personal item or story.

3. Give each student a chance to share a personal belonging or memory with the class.

   - You may wish to provide specific prompts for students to respond to when presenting their chosen item or memory. You may also wish to model a show and tell for students to see what sharing can look like.

4. Allow time for students to ask a few questions or make a few positive comments after each student shares.

5. Celebrate, recognize, or thank each student for sharing.

Teacher Prompts

- Why did you choose to share this with us?

- Why is this special to you?

- What do you think others might not have known about you before this?

- I love hearing why this is important to you.

VARIATIONS

- Do a show and tell with items around the classroom. Students pick their favorite item from the classroom and share why it is their favorite.

- Have students draw or describe their favorite place and do a show and tell about it.

- Ask students to take home a small bag and put five little, inexpensive items in it that represent them in some way. Have students bring their bag back to the classroom and do a show and tell about the items.

Classroom Case Example

Mr. Rogers sets aside time on the last day of each school week for one student to bring in an item or present a memory that is important to them. He lets parents know when it is their child's turn to share and gives reminders as well. Today it is James's turn to share. James has brought in a family cookie recipe. Before James begins sharing with the class, Mr. Rogers reminds him to share what he has brought, where it came from, and why it is important to him. James thoroughly explains all of this about the cookie recipe. He passes the recipe around for other students to see. Then James calls on a few students who have their hands raised to ask him questions or give him positive feedback about the recipe. After James does so, the class together says, "Thank you for sharing, James," and gives him three claps, their customary celebration.

Tips for Success: How to Make Community Building Worthwhile

MAKE THIS A STARTING POINT. Once you have tried a few different activities with a class, you will better understand how best to modify or create activities to build community. Your students' preferences, strengths, and weaknesses as a group will help you plan activities that will help your classroom community grow.

PRIORITIZE IT. Community building is best done regularly to truly strengthen relationships and create change. This means we must prioritize community-building activities in our classrooms, even if they are not valued by those above us in the chain of command. When community-building activities are given a place in the classroom, they can end up saving time because students respect and support one another and generally get along.

PLAY A GAME. Kids need time to just be kids. A great way to build community is to simply play fun games together. Many activities in this chapter can be incorporated or made into a game. When students can play together, they feel more comfortable working together.

CHAPTER 8

STUDENT WELL-BEING SUPPORT ACTIVITIES

As demonstrated by Maslow's theory of the hierarchy of needs, individuals must have their basic needs met before they can progress to higher levels of awareness and learning. This means that students must have their basic needs met if they are to be active participants, if not leaders, in the learning process.

AFFIRMATION CREATION

This activity allows students to write and use positive statements, or affirmations. Each student individually determines what affirmation will work best for them. Self-affirmations are then used in the classroom on a regular basis.

TIME: 5 to 10 minutes

POSSIBLE MATERIALS: Sticky notes or notecards

COMMON APPLICATIONS: Before an assessment, social-emotional learning

Step-by-Step Guide

1. Introduce affirmations to the class and explain what they are.

2. Give examples of self-affirmations and when they may be a good fit for someone. Alternatively, model how you would create your own self affirmations.

3. Brainstorm as a class more examples of affirmations.

4. Prompt students to create a short list of affirmations they believe could be beneficial for them to see and say regularly.

5. Have students place the affirmations somewhere easily accessible to them. They may wish to write them on sticky notes or notecards and place the notes in several places around the room or at home.

6. Remind students when it may be beneficial for them to repeat their affirmations, for example, before an assessment.

Teacher Prompts

- What do you need to remind yourself of?

- What negative self-talk do you use that you can turn on its head?

- When might you need to repeat these affirmations to yourself?

- Try starting with "I am," "I can," "You are," or "You can."

- Where can you put these so that you will see them when you need to?

VARIATIONS

- Give students a chance to memorize one or two of their affirmations. Have them repeat them daily at the same time or in the same place, for example, in front of a classroom mirror.

- Allow students to brainstorm and choose their affirmations to use as a class.

Classroom Case Example

Mrs. Adam begins by introducing students to self-affirmations. She explains that affirmations are positive statements that help you challenge your own negative thoughts. The goal is to retrain your brain to remind yourself of your own strengths. Mrs. Adam then writes a few examples of affirmations on the board, describing when each might be beneficial and including her own anecdotes. Then she asks students what other affirmations they can think of and adds them to the board.

After students have been exposed to many examples, Mrs. Adam prompts students to create their own list of about three affirmations they would like to start using. She gives students plenty of time to think and moves around the room, providing assistance to those struggling to come up with ideas. Mrs. Adam then collects each list to laminate, and she sticks the laminated lists on students' desks as a reference for them.

MINDFUL BREATHING

Mindful breathing involves teaching students breathing exercises, which will allow them to become more mentally and emotionally present in the moment and reduce stress. In this activity, students are taught breathing exercises and when to use them.

TIME: 1 to 5 minutes

POSSIBLE MATERIALS: Breathing exercise cards, demonstration videos

COMMON APPLICATIONS: Before or after stressful events, when students need to calm down, in the calming corner or area of the classroom

Step-by-Step Guide

1. Gather resources for breathing exercises and demonstrations, including either cards or videos.

2. Show students different breathing exercises and tools.

3. Lead students through practice breathing exercises.

4. Discuss when using the exercises could be beneficial.

5. Put the tools somewhere accessible and known to students.

Teacher Prompts

- When we notice we are stressed, we can take a moment to breathe.

- Breathing is a great way to center ourselves and clear our minds.

- You might use a breathing exercise when _____.

- Let's try this breathing exercise together.

- When might it be good to use this exercise?

Classroom Case Example

Mrs. Bell wants to start the school year strong by giving her students tools to cope with stress. One such tool is mindful breathing. As students are diving into more academic concepts and are getting into more conflict with one another, she knows some students' stress levels may start to rise. Mrs. Bell selects a few breathing exercises to teach her students first, including rainbow breathing and belly breathing. Mrs. Bell shows videos to demonstrate these to her students. Then she uses a breathing exercise card to lead them through a practice of each type of breathing. The class then discuss when it could be helpful to use these breathing exercises. After brainstorming together, Mrs. Bell shows students where they can find the breathing exercise cards in the classroom. She explains that they can use these whenever they feel the need, as long as they do not distract their classmates.

MINDSET SWITCH

Mindset switch provides students with the tools to help express and internalize a growth mindset, rather than a fixed mindset. It gives teachers the opportunity to address phrases that are hurtful to the learning environment and replace them with helpful ones.

TIME: 5 to 10 minutes

POSSIBLE MATERIALS: Poster or anchor chart, video

COMMON APPLICATIONS: Beginning of school year, any time students are struggling or not expressing a growth mindset

Step-by-Step Guide

1. Notice or think of common phrases students use that are unproductive, demonstrating a fixed mindset.

2. Tell students that these phrases are unacceptable in your classroom and why.

   - It may be helpful to engage students with a video comparing fixed and growth mindsets.

3. Provide students with alternatives to use in place of these phrases, ones that instead express a growth mindset. This can be done by brainstorming alternatives together.

4. Have students practice using these phrases.

   - You may wish to display a poster with this information.

Teacher Prompts

- Instead, let's say _____.

- I will not allow you to talk about yourself that way.

- You may not be able to *yet*.

- How can we change that to reflect a growth mindset?

- What could we say instead?

VARIATIONS

- Use the mindset switch for students who engage in negative self-talk to help them practice positive self-talk.

- Implement this practice during collaborative learning to help switch the mindset toward the task or toward working as a team.

Classroom Case Example

One of Mr. Hansen's pet peeves is when students say, "I don't get it." Not only does this phrase not demonstrate a growth mindset, but it also doesn't help Mr. Hansen identify what students are struggling to understand. Mr. Hansen begins by telling his students that they are not allowed to use this phrase in the classroom. He explains that this phrase does not convey that students can learn to understand something, and it does not give Mr. Hansen information to help them.

"So we won't be using this phrase in our classroom," Mr. Hansen reiterates. "What could we say instead?" he asks. Students respond with various answers, and Mr. Hansen helps them check whether they are helpful and reflect a growth mindset. If so, he records them on a piece of chart paper. Once students have brainstormed several phrases, Mr. Hansen has students read each of them out together. They then discuss when would be good times to use these phrases and decide to begin practicing using them right away.

CLASS JOB APPLICATIONS

Many teachers have class jobs, allowing their students to develop a sense of responsibility and purpose in their classroom. Class job applications give students the chance to help choose their job and build their confidence.

TIME: 10 to 15 minutes

POSSIBLE MATERIALS: Application page, list or description of class jobs

COMMON APPLICATIONS: Beginning of the year, monthly, quarterly

Application Page Example

CLASS JOB APPLICATION
Name:

1. My first-choice job is _____.

   I would be a good fit for this job because _____

   _____

2. My second-choice job is _____.

   I would be a good fit for this job because _____

   _____

3. My third-choice job is _____.

   I would be a good fit for this job because _____

   _____

4. My fourth-choice job is _____.

   I would be a good fit for this job because _____

   _____

Step-by-Step Guide

1. Determine a list of class jobs for your classroom.

   - Ensure that there are enough jobs for every student, even if that means there are multiples of the same job.

2. Create class job applications.

3. Present students with a list of class jobs and duties.

4. Describe the jobs and allow time for students to ask questions about the jobs.

5. Discuss what might make someone a good fit for a given job (that is, their interests, their goals, or their strengths).

6. Give students the job application to fill out.

7. Assign students jobs according to their application and needs.

Teacher Prompts

- What skills or strengths do you have that mean this job would be a good fit for you?

- What interests do you have that align with this job?

- Each job has a special role to help support our classroom.

- People I have seen be very successful at this job are students who work hard to _____.

VARIATIONS

- Have students create the class job descriptions with you before applying for the jobs.

- Have students create résumés to demonstrate their skills instead of, or in addition to, filling out a job application.

Classroom Case Example

The second week of the school year is about to begin, and Miss Mills wants to assign her students class jobs to give them a sense of purpose and responsibility within their classroom community. She creates a list of jobs she needs done regularly for the class, along with a document of the jobs and their duties. The next day, Miss Mills presents students with the list of class jobs and what they entail. She allows students to ask questions for clarification along the way. After she has reviewed all the jobs, Miss Mills hands out job applications. She explains how to complete an application and how students should use their strengths, skills, and interests to explain why they would be a good fit for a job. Then she gives students time to complete their applications. Later, Miss Mills sorts through the applications to determine what job she will assign each student.

SIGN TAP

This activity allows students to be consistently reminded of something important, whether an encouraging phrase or a class expectation. A sign with a significant motto is hung by the classroom door for students to tap as they enter or exit.

TIME: 30 seconds

POSSIBLE MATERIALS: Laminated sign

COMMON APPLICATIONS: Transitions in or out of the classroom

Step-by-Step Guide

1. Determine, with or without students' help, an important phrase you want students to be reminded of regularly.

2. Create and laminate a sign that clearly displays this phrase.

3. Hang the sign by the classroom door at a height students can reach.

4. Teach students how and when to tap the sign. You may also have students say the phrase as they touch it.

5. Have students consistently tap the sign when entering or exiting the room.

Teacher Prompts

- Think about it as you tap it.
- Remember _____.
- We are all responsible for living by this.

VARIATIONS

- Instead of a phrase, use a picture or symbol that represents something important.

- Use the sign as a display of class rules which students have created and agreed to follow. Tapping the sign serves as a reminder of their duty to follow the rules they were a part of establishing.

Classroom Case Example

Ms. Banks teaches her students that mistakes are wonderful. She instills in her class the value of working hard and trying things, even if that means messing up. Ms. Banks uses an Albert Einstein quote, "You never fail until you stop trying," to remind students that persevering is the most important element of success.

Ms. Banks makes a poster of this quote and hangs it beside the entrance to her classroom. She teaches her students to tap the sign each time they enter the classroom.

Tips for Success: How to Provide the Best Well-Being Support

TEACH SOCIAL-EMOTIONAL SKILLS DIRECTLY. Not all school districts provide the resources or build in the time for social-emotional learning. But even just incorporating the direct teaching of social-emotional skills in a lesson once a week can help students learn specific social-emotional skills. Although these skills are not always valued within our school systems, they are a major part of student-centered learning as they are necessary in the outside world.

ENLIST THE HELP OF SUPPORT STAFF, GUEST SPEAKERS, AND FAMILY. A great way to help students apply well-being skills to their lives is to expose them to well-being support in and outside the classroom. Giving students opportunities to check in with and learn from other adults in the school building can give them a well-rounded school experience. Inviting guest speakers to discuss how they take care of themselves within their lifestyle and career field can give students new tools and show them real-world applications of self-care. Finally, keeping students' families in the loop on what well-being skills students are working on can help students practice these skills at home.

FILL THE NEED. Although all student well-being activities can be beneficial, some may be more relevant to students at a given time. For example, if students are struggling to cope with their emotions, mindful breathing may be a useful next activity. Observe student issues that arise, and use student-centered activities to help address them.

CHAPTER 9

ACTIVITY RESOURCES

Many resources are available to assist you in implementing student-centered learning activities. Resources to engage students, promote collaboration, and allow students to take the initiative in their learning pair perfectly with student-centered activities. Many resources, including those in this chapter, can also be helpful in collecting data or allowing students to demonstrate their learning. Be conscious of how you use these resources in your classroom, as many resources can also be used in teacher-centered instruction. Before using a resource, ask yourself these questions:

- Am I using this to give my students tools to apply in their lives?

- Are my students able to take ownership of their learning?

- Are my students engaged?

- Can my students make choices or take the initiative with this?

- Are my students able to explore and try this on their own and at their own pace?

- Can my students use this to work together or provide feedback to each other?

- What do I want my students to gain from this?

Following are some of my favorite resources that can accompany student-centered activities.

Blooket

USES: Independent exploration and practice, demonstration of learning, collaboration

DESCRIPTION: Blooket is a skills or concept practice online game. Students join a Blooket game hosted by either the teacher or another student, and they answer questions to practice or demonstrate learning regarding a learning target. There are a variety of game mode options, some of which allow students to collaborate as a team. Teachers can create their own questions or use one of the already created games. Game hosts can determine the game's time or question length, or how much must be correct for the game to end. Students receive immediate feedback when they answer a question, as they are told whether their answer is correct, and if not, what the correct answer is. I love to use Blooket because it is naturally engaging for students and because students can work through the questions at their own pace. I often use it to help students practice skills, collect formative data, or review content.

GRADE LEVELS: K–6   **WEB ADDRESS:** blooket.com
ACCESS: Free

BrainPOP or BrainPOP Jr.

USES: Instruction, independent exploration and practice, research

DESCRIPTION: BrainPOP and its junior version provide animated video lessons and accompanying content on a wide variety of topics. After students watch the video lessons, they can engage with the content through a variety of exercises. These include arranging concepts in a graphic organizer, quizzing their understanding, learning vocabulary, making connections via reading, and playing a game. Each lesson includes the standards it addresses. The site also includes detailed lesson plans to accompany each video lesson. Some of BrainPOP's major benefits, along with engagement, are that its content allows for a high level of interaction and its lesson plans usually include student-centered activities, such as projects.

GRADE LEVELS: K–6   **WEB ADDRESS:** brainpop.com
ACCESS: Paid subscription

Breakout EDU

USES: Collaboration, independent exploration and practice

DESCRIPTION: Breakout EDU is the ultimate hub of digital escape rooms. The site includes digital breakout and physical breakout kit options for you to use on almost every topic imaginable. Students use critical thinking skills to apply their growing knowledge in new and interesting ways. Not only are students super engaged with the breakout but they are also challenged. This is especially helpful in promoting a growth mindset. Teachers have access to the answers, as well as hints they can give at their discretion. Students can be assigned breakouts individually, or in a small or large group for collaborative learning. I especially love to use breakouts from this site for individuals or small groups of students who need to be challenged or receive extensions on any given topic. Once students adapt to the breakout problem-solving process, they can't get enough!

GRADE LEVELS: K–6 **WEB ADDRESS:** breakoutedu.com

ACCESS: Paid subscription

Ducksters

USES: Instruction, research

DESCRIPTION: Ducksters is an informative, kid-friendly site. Most of the site is a seemingly endless amount of articles about almost any social studies topic. Many articles have an audio recording attached so that students can listen to information as well as read it. Each article also includes a brief quiz to review the ideas covered. Other features of the site include content-related games and activities such as word searches. My favorite way to use this site is to provide it as a source to students for research. It is accessible to many different levels of readers and is thorough in its discussion of topics. Many of my students who pick topics for which it is difficult to find a good source can find plenty of kid-friendly information on Ducksters.

GRADE LEVELS: 2–6 **WEB ADDRESS:** ducksters.com

ACCESS: Free

Edpuzzle

USES: Instruction, demonstration of learning

DESCRIPTION: Edpuzzle is an incredible resource for the virtual or flipped classroom, wherein the direct instruction takes place outside of class time. It allows educators to take videos, including YouTube videos or self-recorded videos, and make them interactive. Educators can build in pause points in the video for students to read a note, do an activity, or answer a question. Edpuzzle records data of questions answered for students who sign in. What I love about Edpuzzle is that it allows you to personalize engaging instruction for your students while also allowing students to work on and demonstrate learning. Some of my students, as a demonstration of mastery, have even created their own Edpuzzle interactive videos to teach a concept.

GRADE LEVELS: K–6 **WEB ADDRESS:** edpuzzle.com

ACCESS: Free for as many as twenty videos in storage, paid subscription for additional storage

Epic!

USES: Research, independent exploration and practice, instruction, demonstration of learning, social-emotional learning

DESCRIPTION: The digital library available on Epic is diverse in reading level, accessibility, content, and length. Epic allows educators to create a class, or import their Google Classroom, and track their students' online reading. Teachers can assign or send books to students as reading recommendations or for instructional use. Many books also have quizzes that can be assigned. Alternatively, educators can write their own quizzes. Some books are Epic originals, but most are ones that you could find elsewhere. Educators can sort books by genre, topic, or reading level. Read-to-me books and audiobooks are also available. Students can also use similar categories to search for books. I often use Epic to allow my students to explore and find an engaging independent reading book. Epic can also be a great tool for research as educators can create collections of books to send to their students.

GRADE LEVELS: K–6   **WEB ADDRESS:** getepic.com

ACCESS: Free school access

Flipgrid

USES: Collaborative learning, demonstration of learning, social-emotional learning

DESCRIPTION: Flipgrid is a unique video discussion site that allows students to create and post videos. Educators can either limit or expand a wide variety of settings that students have access to when they create their videos in response to a prompt. Video creators can record themselves, their screens, or just their voices, as well as edit their videos before posting. Students can view all other students' posts and respond to them. I see Flipgrid as a safer, more positive, and educational version of social media. Students are incredibly engaged as they create content to which their classmates have access. The uses of Flipgrid in the classroom are truly limited only by your imagination.

GRADE LEVELS: K–6   **WEB ADDRESS:** info.flipgrid.com

ACCESS: Free

Flocabulary

USES: Instruction, independent exploration and practice, social-emotional learning

DESCRIPTION: Flocabulary is a virtual library of educational music videos. The engaging songs and accompanying videos describe and explain concepts thoroughly, understandably, and memorably. Students can sing along to music videos and then use the information presented to help them with a variety of corresponding activities, including vocabulary practice, quizzes, and reading and response. One of my favorite features is the quick review, which presents key questions for class discussion on the topic. Students love the videos and remember the information because of the engaging musical display. I often reference phrases from the songs and replay the videos throughout my students' time learning about a concept.

GRADE LEVELS: K–6 **WEB ADDRESS:** flocabulary.com

ACCESS: Paid subscription

Google Classroom

USES: Instruction, demonstration of learning, access to other resources, collaboration

DESCRIPTION: Google Classroom is the ultimate virtual learning platform. It can be organized so that students can find and gain access to resources and assignments. Not only is it great for encouraging student digital literacy, but it is also a simple way to differentiate learning, as educators can assign students items according to their individual needs. Google Classroom allows teachers to create quizzes, Google Docs, and Google Slides, and attach them to posts so that students may view them, edit them, or work collaboratively on them. It also gives students the ability to create and attach their own Google Drive items. Posts can include links to other resources for instruction or research. I use Google Classroom regularly to provide my students with resources, collaborate with them on their learning, and allow them to collaborate with each other. It is the ultimate tool for in-person or virtual learning.

GRADE LEVELS: K–6 **WEB ADDRESS:** classroom.google.com

ACCESS: Free school access, paid subscription for additional features

Google Drive

USES: Collaboration, demonstration of learning, independent exploration and practice

DESCRIPTION: Going hand in hand with Google Classroom is Google Drive, which allows students to create a variety of products, including documents, drawings, and presentations. Students love working on their devices, and teachers have direct and consistent access to student work once it is shared with them. Teachers and students alike can comment on others' work to collaborate and provide feedback. I love that I can constantly see and check on students' in-progress work. Google Drive's platform makes it easy for me to provide students with feedback and to present student examples.

GRADE LEVELS: K–6 **WEB ADDRESS:** drive.google.com

ACCESS: Free

Greg Tang Math

USES: Independent exploration and practice

DESCRIPTION: Greg Tang's site helps students practice number sense and critical thinking while giving teachers resources to provide these skills as well. The site comprises a series of online games for students to practice various math skills. It also has printable resources for teachers, including logic puzzles. I use this site to help students engage with problem-solving and develop their growth mindset. Many of the games have levels and settings so that students can start practicing at their own pace and current point of understanding.

GRADE LEVELS: K–6   **WEB ADDRESS:** tangmath.com

ACCESS: Free, some paid resources

Jamboard

USES: Collaboration, instruction

DESCRIPTION: Jamboard is a collaborative digital whiteboard. Although it is just a whiteboard, it has many uses. A big benefit of this online platform is how easy it is to use for collaboration. Jamboard allows students and teachers to display information, work out problems, view others' work, and provide feedback. A teacher can share one Jamboard for the entire class to use, giving each student a page to work on. Alternatively, the teacher can display an anchor chart on their own board. Creators can easily type, insert clip art images, draw, or write on their Jamboard. I love to use Jamboard as an option for students to create a virtual poster on which to demonstrate learning, especially because it can be shared with me, just as a Google Doc could.

GRADE LEVELS: K–6   **WEB ADDRESS:** jamboard.google.com

ACCESS: Free

Kahoot!

USES: Independent exploration and practice, collaboration

DESCRIPTION: Similar to Blooket but a little less complex, Kahoot! is a game-based question-asking platform. Students can either collaborate or compete in answering questions. The teacher displays the questions one at a time on the board, and students answer and then have the correct answer revealed to them once everyone has answered or the time is up (depending on the game's settings). The benefit of everyone answering the same question at the same time is the great opportunity this allows for discussion after each question. The data displayed immediately after each question help the teacher determine what should be discussed. I also love that the data displayed after the game finishes allow me to see what each player individually missed, giving me a better picture of what this student understands. The site includes many games, but teachers can also create their own game or edit a game to personalize it for their students and learning targets.

GRADE LEVELS: K–6   **WEB ADDRESS:** kahoot.com

ACCESS: Free, paid subscription for additional features

Kiddle

USES: Research, instruction, independent exploration

DESCRIPTION: I think of Kiddle as a kid-appropriate Google. Kiddle is a search engine that allows students to search for a topic and view a variety of screened resources. Though not all sites Kiddle finds are at an elementary reading level, many are. I like to use Kiddle as a research tool for my students because I know I do not have to worry about the content they will find.

GRADE LEVELS: K–4   **WEB ADDRESS:** kiddle.co

ACCESS: Free

Learning for Justice

USES: Instruction, access to other resources, social-emotional learning

DESCRIPTION: Learning for Justice is a free educator resource site. Its content explores powerful, relevant, and valuable content concerning social justice. Resources on the site include detailed lesson plans, student texts, student project prompts, and even printable posters. Many resources can be used to address multiple learning targets at once. The site's thorough discussions and real-life applications are a boon when planning for the classroom.

GRADE LEVELS: K–6, mainly 3–6   **WEB ADDRESS:** learningforjustice.org

ACCESS: Free

National Geographic Kids

USES: Research, instruction, independent exploration

DESCRIPTION: Based on the *National Geographic Kids* magazine, this site is an encyclopedia of fun and interesting facts about a plethora of topics. Students can use the site to explore, research, and test their knowledge when it comes to many scientific phenomena, creatures, and locations around the world. Articles on the site are nicely outlined and wholesome for kid-friendly access. Many other resources, including videos and quizzes, are also available on the site. Science, especially when it comes to animals, is naturally engaging for most students. As many students like to explore and research this topic, I often recommend Nat Geo Kids as a resource.

GRADE LEVELS: 2–6 **WEB ADDRESS:** kids.nationalgeographic.com

ACCESS: Free

Nearpod

USES: Instruction, demonstration of learning

DESCRIPTION: Similar to Edpuzzle, but with more glitz and glamour, Nearpod allows teachers to create interactive video lessons and pair them with other resources for the entire virtual lesson. It can be useful in a flipped classroom setting, as students are introduced to the content completely through one Nearpod lesson and its links. Nearpod has many original instructional videos and also allows teachers to use YouTube videos. With Nearpod, teachers can string together a variety of learning activities, including interactive videos, slideshows, web links, and more, to create a lesson. Educators choose the order in which activities are done, as well as the other activities to which they are linked, so they must be careful to include student choice and personalization when possible.

GRADE LEVELS: 2–6 **WEB ADDRESS:** nearpod.com

ACCESS: Free, paid subscription options

Numberock

USES: Instruction

DESCRIPTION: This collection of music videos is used to display math concepts and strategies in engaging and memorable ways. Using the videos, students take ownership of the information presented as they recall and sing the words to the songs. Added benefits of the paid site are downloadable lesson plans, practice, games, and anchor charts, as well as digital self-graded task cards for Google Classroom. I use Numberock videos when introducing a math concept and repeatedly throughout the concept to give students a great reference point for the topic. My students will sing the songs to help each other out on specific tasks.

GRADE LEVELS: K–5 **WEB ADDRESS:** numberock.com

ACCESS: Paid subscription, most videos available free on YouTube

Padlet

USES: Collaboration, instruction, demonstration of learning

DESCRIPTION: Padlet is a digital bulletin board tool. Using the site, teachers and students can set up a virtual board with a variety of setting choices. They can share the board with others to collaborate or present information. Posts on each board can look like simple sticky notes or can include other media, such as photos, links, or drawings. Users can also have the option to respond to each other's posts via words, likes, or a rating system. I have used Padlet to create a KWL (what students know, want to learn, and what they have learned) chart and to share reading responses. My favorite uses have been when students created elaborate final projects with Padlet to demonstrate their learning. Padlet can be used to create interesting portfolios or graphic organizers. It can also be used to track inquiry-based learning projects. The possibilities for Padlet when it comes to student-centered learning are impossible to count.

GRADE LEVELS: 1–6   **WEB ADDRESS:** padlet.com

ACCESS: Free, paid subscription for more than a few saved pages

PBS Kids

USES: Independent exploration and practice, instruction, social-emotional learning, collaboration

DESCRIPTION: PBS Kids features educational games and videos that are engaging and fun for students. Students can use the site to explore new concepts or practice with familiar ones. Younger students in particular love that the site's content centers on characters from some of their favorite shows. Many show clips can be viewed during instruction and help students connect their learning to life outside the classroom. I personally like that most of the games are not timed, so students can coach others or receive assistance in working through a problem before it disappears.

GRADE LEVELS: K–3   **WEB ADDRESS:** pbskids.org

ACCESS: Free

PBS Learning Media

USES: Instruction, research

DESCRIPTION: This site is a library of teaching resources, including videos, lesson plans, games, and other activities. All teaching resources are categorized according to learning standards, ideal grade level, and topics. Most of the resources incorporate more than one content area, making it well-rounded, true-to-life learning. Some of the site's lessons are already interactive and ready for digital assignment as well. The diversity and unique sources on the site make it a go-to resource when planning lessons. I have used the site on several occasions to plan projects and assign lessons that allow students to have choices and investigate.

GRADE LEVELS: K–6   **WEB ADDRESS:** pbslearningmedia.org

ACCESS: Free

Pear Deck

USES: Instruction, demonstration of learning, independent exploration and practice

DESCRIPTION: Pear Deck is an add-on for Google Slides that allows teachers to differentiate extremely well for their students. Using Pear Deck, educators can easily embed informative and engaging features, including formative assessments and interactive questions. Another brilliant aspect of Pear Deck is that you can make the presentation either student-paced or instructor-paced, depending on whether you are using it for whole-group instruction or independent exploration and practice. If teachers are making the presentation student-paced, they can add audio recordings, descriptions, and examples for their students as they review the content on their own. In my classroom, I have used Pear Deck a lot with whole-group instruction to make sure every student's voice is heard and every student can feel that learning is extremely accessible. Each class member has their individual device out and is interacting with others and the learning as we go along. Pear Deck can provide that perfect balance between student autonomy, collaboration, and direct instruction.

GRADE LEVELS: K–6   **WEB ADDRESS:** peardeck.com

ACCESS: Free, paid subscription for additional features

PebbleGo and PebbleGo Next

USES: Instruction, research

DESCRIPTION: PebbleGo is an extremely accessible online encyclopedia. The site has more than 1,500 articles in five subject areas. Users can search the site or click through categories to find an article on a topic of their choice. Each article comes with the options for text-to-speech, the dictionary definition for most words, activities, videos, and other features. The depth of information covered in each topic and a set of well-organized subtopics make it the perfect site for research or student exploration. Anytime I would like students to research something, PebbleGo is a preferred resource.

GRADE LEVELS: K–3 (PebbleGo), 3–5 (PebbleGo Next)   **WEB ADDRESS:** pebblego.com

ACCESS: Paid subscription

Prodigy

USES: Independent practice, instruction, demonstration of learning, collaboration

DESCRIPTION: Prodigy is an addictive math gaming site for students. Students set themselves up as characters in a mystical world and engage in magic battles for coins and pets. Despite its fantastical premise, students answer math questions in their battles. There's no limit to the number of problems, but the greater the number of correct answers, the better the outcome of the battles. Teachers can choose to let their students engage in free play on Prodigy (many of them do so at home as well) or give them Prodigy assignments. Students don't know when they are given assignments in the game. But if students have joined an educator's class and use a code when they log in and play from school, the math problems for their battles will all include the range of skills their teacher has designated. My students are always extremely engaged with Prodigy. I adore the site as my students have fun, make choices, think critically, and practice math skills. This is all while I am able to differentiate the content for individual students and get individual student data regarding specific math standards.

GRADE LEVELS: 1–5   **WEB ADDRESS:** prodigygame.com

ACCESS: Free, paid premium membership for students or families

Quandary

USES: Independent exploration and practice, social-emotional learning

DESCRIPTION: This unique game site is based on ethical decision-making. Its engaging premise is that players are going to a new planet to set up a colony. Along the way, students have to use critical thinking, empathy, perspective-taking skills, and decision-making skills to work for the best possible outcome for everyone. The site also includes curriculum and game support materials to help educators drive home the points learned in the game. Many students also benefit simply from discussions surrounding the game, as it presents great scenarios to spark conversations about real-world problems.

GRADE LEVELS: 5–6   **WEB ADDRESS:** quandarygame.org

ACCESS: Free

ReadWorks

USES: Instruction, independent exploration and practice, demonstration of learning, research

DESCRIPTION: ReadWorks provides content, curriculum, and tools for reading skills and strategies. The passages and questions presented on the site allow students to explore many topics. Questions that accompany the passages benefit not only students' reading comprehension but also their critical thinking skills. Teachers can assign articles virtually or they can print out any of the passages for students' use. I like to use Readworks passages as examples of specific types of works and to model specific reading skills. The variety of topics available allows me to help students engage with what they are reading and connect it to their lives.

GRADE LEVELS: K–6   **WEB ADDRESS:** readworks.org

ACCESS: Free

Starfall

USES: Instruction, independent exploration and practice

DESCRIPTION: Starfall is a simple online game and practice platform. The site is divided into categories according to grade level and content. Students can play games and read stories to practice numbers sense and reading decoding skills. Though the practice is straightforward, the game setup keeps students engaged in learning. Particularly for reading, I like to use Starfall to get students interested and motivated in their practice. Many students go on the site at home by choice for practice, which is a bonus.

GRADE LEVELS: K–3   **WEB ADDRESS:** starfall.com

ACCESS: Free, paid subscription for additional content

Teachers Pay Teachers

USES: Access to resources for demonstrations of learning, instruction, independent exploration and practice

DESCRIPTION: Tread carefully when using Teachers Pay Teachers, as resources may not always be completely accurate or useful. But the site has an impressive, seemingly endless, amount of resources. Teacher-created lessons, games, projects, escape rooms, practice, assessments, puzzles, and other tools can all be found regarding pretty much any learning goal. I particularly love to use Teachers Pay Teachers to find the parts for collaborative learning activities. I also like knowing I'm supporting other teachers with my purchases.

GRADE LEVELS: K–6   **WEB ADDRESS:** teacherspayteachers.com

ACCESS: Free, many resources must be purchased

Wonderopolis

USES: Independent exploration and practice, instruction, research, social-emotional learning

DESCRIPTION: Wonderopolis is an exciting website full of what kids wonder about and the answers. Articles on the site address questions, many of which have been submitted by students, answering them in a kid-friendly manner. The articles often include read-to-me features and knowledge checks for readers. Students can visit the site either with the intent to explore or to find the answer to something specific. There is a wide range of concepts on the site, but most are related to science, social-emotional issues, or social studies. In my classroom, we use Wonderopolis for research, reading, and other exploration. I like to use the site because it promotes the idea that learning can happen anytime, anywhere.

GRADE LEVELS: K–6   **WEB ADDRESS:** wonderopolis.org

ACCESS: Free

YouTube

USES: Instruction, research

DESCRIPTION: Though YouTube can seem like a scary pit of unfiltered video content, it is an amazing resource when used correctly and monitored appropriately. YouTube is an expansive video library, which can allow students to gain access to information about different ideas and instructions for various creations. Students can use the site to learn multiple ways to attempt something, research a topic of their interest, or review material in a different light. I use YouTube videos regularly in my instruction to engage students and present them with information in a new manner. Not only do students love and remember YouTube videos, but they return to them and later use them on their own.

GRADE LEVELS: K–6   **WEB ADDRESS:** youtube.com or youtubekids.com

ACCESS: Free

Pick a few resources from this list to incorporate into your student-centered learning activities and make those activities that much more effective.

CHAPTER 10

CONCLUSION

Think about the traditional teacher-centered model compared with the student-centered model. Reflect on your classroom. Where does it fall on the spectrum of teacher-centered to student-centered? For many of us, our classroom environment is more teacher-centered than not, though we might incorporate some student-centered elements. But the more we move toward student-centered learning, the better our teaching will be—for both our students and ourselves.

PROS AND CONS OF STUDENT-CENTERED AND TEACHER-CENTERED APPROACHES

Though there are pros and cons to both approaches, the benefits of the student-centered approach for students—and for teachers—are significantly greater than those of teacher-centered learning. Make the conscious choice to move in the direction that is better for your students.

STUDENT-CENTERED APPROACH	
Pros for Students	**Cons for Students**
• Engagement	• Adapting to changes in classroom noise level
• Ownership and agency	• Relying on other students for collaboration
• Application of learning outside the classroom	• Classroom management adjustments
• Development of critical thinking and problem-solving skills	
• More well-rounded education	
• Exploration of interests and passions	
• Communication and collaboration skills	
• Positive relationships	
• Establish a growth mindset	
• Autonomy	
• Better student outcomes	
• Higher student engagement	
• Meet more student needs	
• Less planning	
• Collaboration with students	
• Positive learning environment	

TEACHER-CENTERED APPROACH	
Pros for Students	**Cons for Students**
• Students know to focus on the teacher	• Most learning comes from one source: the teacher
• Extremely predictable	• May get bored easily
• Clear, specific lesson plans	• Minimal to no choice
• Control	• Limited opportunities to develop many important life skills, including critical thinking and collaboration
	• Overly dependent on teacher
	• Pressure to keep lessons interesting
	• Minimal student progress and growth
	• "Hand-holding" of students
	• Dull learning environment

STUDENT-CENTERED LESSON-PLANNING GUIDE

You might be feeling motivated to start making your classroom more student-centered but be undecided about which activities to begin implementing first. Here's my suggestion for beginning the process of student-centered lesson planning.

1. Start with relationships, personalization, and application.

If you aren't ready to make big changes to your classroom planning, start with the basics. Though you've heard it often, relationships with students do make a world of difference. Building a positive, individualized relationship with each of your students doesn't take much time or planning. Most of the activities in Chapter 6 on building the teacher–student relationship are brief and require little preparation. Making your students feel noticed can also be built into the school day by ensuring there are plenty of opportunities for each student's voice to be heard.

Personalization is another simple way to make your students feel seen and engage them with learning. Adding student names or interests to a math problem, writing sample, or reading passage takes minimal time and energy. But it is one step in the direction of making your classroom more student-centered. When a student hears their name or is getting to work with a topic they enjoy, they are much more likely to be mentally and emotionally present in the learning experience. Even just adding pictures or items around your classroom that reflect students' individuality is a great way to help personalize their learning environment, allowing them to feel at home in the classroom.

Finally, many teachers find it easy to emphasize the applications of what students are learning. This is something we often mean to do as teachers, but it often falls by the wayside when we plan lessons. But it is key in student-centered learning to give students the knowledge and ability to apply the skills they are learning. Stating when students might use what they are learning, or even better, having students actually apply the skills in a real-life situation, can give students buy-in to their learning. This can go along with personalization by presenting students with scenarios that you know they have come across or would be interested in. Tweak some of your examples to reflect the real world or describe the learning target when you use a skill. Including these things in our lesson plans can make our teaching so much more student-centered.

2. Pick a couple of activities to master at a time.

As teachers, we are pulled in so many directions that we often try to master too many skills at once. Set a goal for yourself to get really good at two of your favorite activities in this book. Include them in your lesson plans weekly or daily. Work out the kinks and adapt the activities to best fit your classroom. Once you have mastered these activities, add another one. I suggest picking one whole-group activity and one small-group or conference activity to begin implementing first.

3. Observe and discuss with an expert teacher.

Expert teachers are already doing a lot of student-centered teaching, even if they don't recognize it as such. If possible, ask your administrators for the opportunity to observe an expert teacher at work. Go in with the intent to notice the ways they are creating student-centered learning. Take note of the language and approaches they use with their students. Even just talking to an expert teacher about how they address areas you are struggling to master can provide you with meaningful insight.

4. Let lines blur between content areas.

Whether you collaborate with a team or plan lessons on your own, make it a goal to encourage students to learn anytime, anywhere. This means allowing math skills to be used in reading, reading skills to be used in social studies, and so on. If at all possible, create large overarching projects or inquiries that can encompass the learning targets of multiple subject areas. These activities can include other activities within them. For example, if students are working on creating a series of letters from the perspective of someone who lived during the Civil War, you could include a model mini-lesson on how to write in letter format.

5. Hand over the reins to your students.

As much as you can, let students determine their own goals, demonstrations of learning, and areas of exploration. Often certain aspects of our curriculum are dictated by those above us in the school hierarchy. But when you can allow for more student ownership and choice, let it happen. It may get messy, and it may take some adaptation on your part and theirs, but it will allow students to learn more and develop the important skill of critical thinking. Outline your lesson plans with the standards, learning targets, materials, and learning activities—and that's it. Don't outline every element of the lesson in rigid detail, but rather adapt to your students' needs and preferences throughout the class session.

LESSON-PLANNING OUTLINE

Standards:	Learning Targets: • • •
Materials:	Learning Activities: 1. 2. 3.
Notes or Reminders:	Assessment of Learning Targets:

FINAL THOUGHTS

My hope with this book is to make student-centered learning more accessible to the elementary classroom. When we feel like we are herding a classroom of cats, trying something "new" is not always first on our list, even if we know that it can benefit our students. But creating a student-centered learning environment starts with just one activity. If we make the effort to include a student-centered activity in our daily lesson plans, the result will be well worth the time and energy it takes, and may even make the cats a little easier to herd. By making our classrooms student-centered, we are giving our students the skills and knowledge they need to succeed in the world, which ultimately is the goal of teaching.

We know how much we as educators already have on our plate. Our students and their needs are just part of what we are asked to attend to daily, and the load has only grown heavier in recent years. The little things we do for our students each and every day, though, are what ultimately shift our classrooms into student-centered spaces and thus world-changing environments. Despite whatever else might come our way, we must take on the responsibility to ensure we provide certain student-centered aspects of learning in our classroom every day.

SAFETY AND TRUST. The relationship and environment we create for each of our students must foster security and ease. Getting to know our students on a very individual level is a key element of student-centered learning because it allows students to be in the best mindset for learning. As Maslow's hierarchy of needs suggests, humans must have their physiological, safety, and social needs met in order to process higher-order thinking. We must take the time and energy to understand what our students need and provide that for them when possible. Establishing a relationship and place of safety and trust will allow students to learn and grow. For some of our students, it may be the only place they receive this kind of unconditional support, and we must make every minute of it count.

COLLABORATION AND COMMUNITY. Collaboration with others and participation in the community are not only important life skills for students but are also components of a better-functioning society. Through student-centered learning, students collaborate and build community in a way that reflects society outside their school building. The tools for clear communication, problem-solving, and fulfillment of duty must all be experienced directly in a student-centered classroom. Regularly providing students with opportunities to work with and support one another goes back to making students feel safe, and it also gives them a sense of purpose and determination. They can realize that what they do affects those around them, whether in a positive or a negative manner.

CRITICAL THINKING AND APPLICATION OF LEARNING. Finally, we must provide students with regular opportunities to creatively apply skills to new problems. The skill of critical thinking is what makes our students take their learning beyond an assessment and beyond the classroom. Students who understand when and how to apply their learning have more ownership of their learning and can problem-solve new situations. Ultimately, this allows them to develop the grit that makes for success in life. Students can face a task, believe in their ability to accomplish it, and learn from their failures.

I hope you find that the activities in this book make it easier to regularly provide time and opportunities for these aspects of learning. Our incredibly challenging, important, and rewarding work is reflected in what our students take with them each day. Their futures, and the future of our society, rely on us giving them these tools to succeed.

BIBLIOGRAPHY

Asoodeh, Mohammad H., Mohammad B. Asoodeh, and Maryam Zarepour. "The Impact of Student-Centered Learning on Academic Achievement and Social Skills." *Procedia: Social and Behavioral Sciences* (September 1, 2012). https://www.sciencedirect.com/science/article/pii/S187704281201289X.

Bell, S. "Project-Based Learning for the 21st Century: Skills for the Future." *The Clearing House*, 83(2) (February 2010): 39—43.

Deye, Sunny. *NCSL Student-Centered Learning Commission: National Conference of State Legislatures*, 2021. https://www.ncsl.org/research/education/ncsl-student-centered-learning-commission.aspx.

Friedlaender, Diane, Dion Burns, Heather Lewis-Charp, Channa Cook-Harvey, Xinhua Zheng, and Linda Darling-Hammond. "Student-Centered Schools: Closing the Opportunity Gap." Stanford Center for Opportunity Policy in Education. November 30, 2013. https://eric.ed.gov/?id=ED611377.

Kaput, Krista. *Evidence for Student-Centered Learning*. St. Paul, MN: Education Evolving, 2017. https://www.educationevolving.org.

Lathan, Joseph, PhD. "Complete Guide to Teacher-Centered vs. Student-Centered Learning." University of San Diego, accessed April 30, 2021. https://onlinedegrees.sandiego.edu/teacher-centered-vs-student-centered-learning/.

Overby, Kimberly. "Student-Centered Learning." *ESSAI* 9 (April 1, 2011): 109–12.

Pane, John F., Elizabeth D. Steiner, Matthew D. Baird, and Laura S. Hamilton. 2015. *Continued Progress: Promising Evidence on Personalized Learning*. Santa Monica, CA: RAND Corporation.

ACKNOWLEDGMENTS

Thank you to all the amazing teachers out there, including my coworkers and college professors, for inspiring me and working to do the best for your students each and every day. Thank you to my students—present, past, and future—for being the reason why I do what I do. Most of all, thank you to my family, especially my husband and son, for supporting and loving me through my wild endeavors.

ABOUT THE AUTHOR

Erin Ellis is a third-grade teacher who loves spending each day working to provide a more student-centered learning environment for her silly, unique, and caring students. Her research on growth mindset, assessment-capable learners, and student-centered approaches has given her insight into how effective student-centered learning can be at creating long-term student success.

Her practical experience teaching and writing curriculum allows her to describe activities that are truly applicable to elementary teaching and its challenges. Erin has a bachelor's degree in psychology and a master's degree in elementary education. She has experience working in a variety of schools in Missouri, where she lives with her wonderful husband, adorable son, and several fluffy creatures.